The
WILD WORLD of the
FUTURE

FIREFLY BOOKS

Contents

The Wild World of the Future is a book about evolution. Inside, you will find out how present-day science helps us to imagine our world as it might be in the future. You will meet amazing creatures that could one day exist, and follow their struggle for survival in hostile lands and against terrifying predators.

INTRODUCTION

4   Changing world
Earth's plates and how they move

8   Our world today
Climates, habitats and animals

14   Understanding evolution
Why animals change and adapt

20   Imagining the future
Create your own future creature!

5 MILLION YEARS

22   5 million years map
Our world, 5 million years in the future

24   North European Ice
Gannetwhales, snowstalkers and shagrats

28   The Mediterranean Basin
Cryptile lizards, scrofas and grykens

34   The Amazon Grasslands
Babookaris, rattlebacks and carakillers

38   The North American Desert
Deathgleaners

All glossary entries in this book are marked in **bold**.

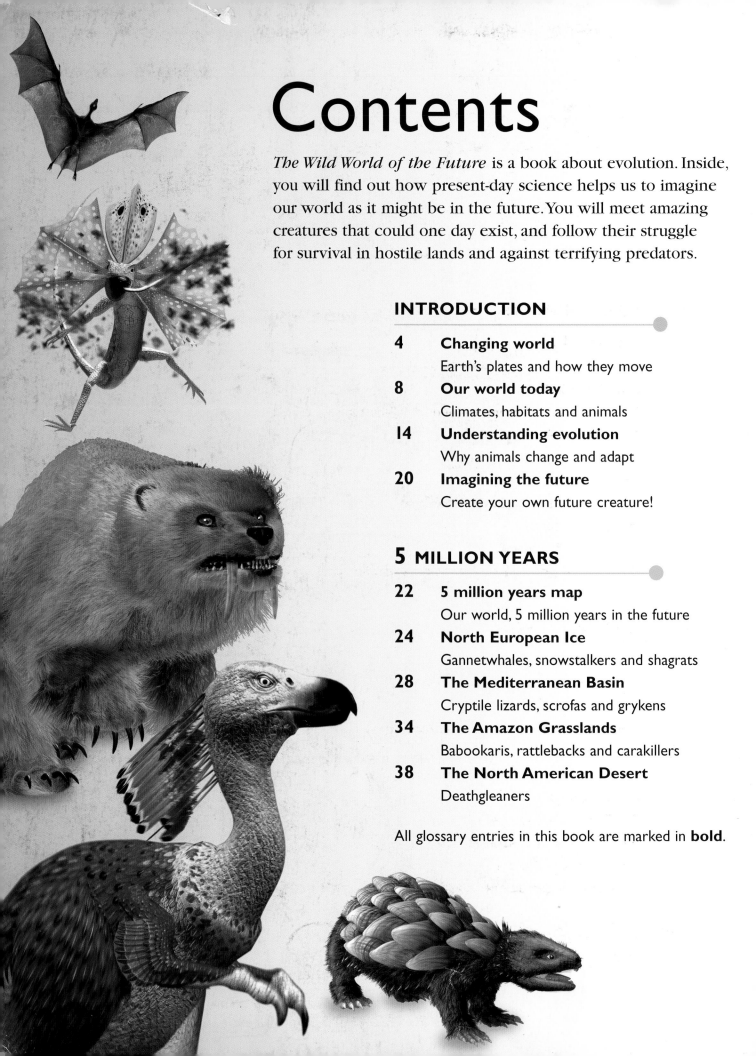

100 MILLION YEARS

40   **100 million years map**
Our world, 100 million years in the future

42   **The Shallow Seas**
Reef gliders, ocean phantoms and spindletroopers

48   **The Bengal Swamp**
Lurkfish, toratons and swampuses

54   **The Antarctic Forest**
Roachcutters, spitfire birds, falconflies
and spitfire beetles

58   **The Great Plateau**
Great blue windrunners, silver spiders and poggles

200 MILLION YEARS

64   **200 million years map**
Our world, 200 million years in the future

66   **The Central Desert**
Terabytes, garden worms and slickribbons

72   **The Global Ocean**
Silverswimmers, ocean flish, sharkopaths
and rainbow squids

80   **The Rainshadow Desert**
Desert hoppers and bumblebeetles

84   **The Northern Forest**
Forest flish, megasquids and squibbons

90   Creature profiles
92   Glossary
94   Index

Changing world

Although you may not realize it, our world is constantly changing. Ocean waves wear away at cliffs, rivers carve out deep **valleys**, and wind and rain batter mountainsides. Sometimes, there is a dramatic change. Violent earthquakes crack open the ground. Volcanoes erupt, spewing out red hot lava, or liquid rock. These natural events are the result of movements that begin deep inside Earth.

Earth's plates

Earth's **continents** and oceans sit upon huge pieces of Earth's **crust** called **plates**. The plates fit together like a massive jigsaw puzzle. They float on top of Earth's **mantle**, like rafts on water.

INSIDE EARTH

Earth is made up of different layers, like an onion. The outer layer of rock is called the crust. Beneath, there is a thick layer called the mantle, with brittle rock near the top and molten, or melted, rock beneath. The core is at the center of Earth. The outer core is molten metal and the inner core is a ball of incredibly hot, solid metal.

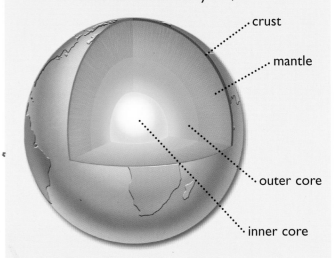

crust

mantle

outer core

inner core

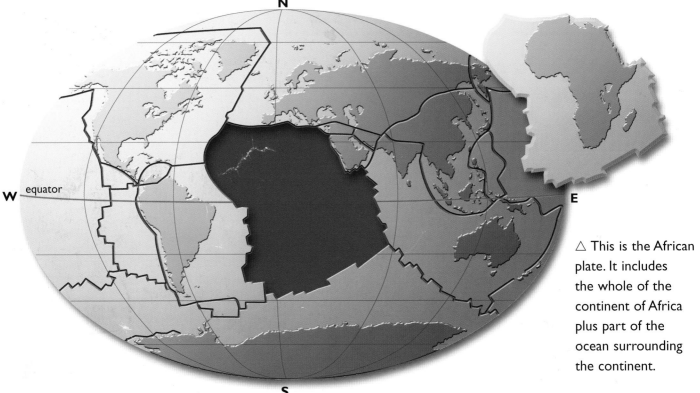

N

W

equator

E

S

△ This is the African plate. It includes the whole of the continent of Africa plus part of the ocean surrounding the continent.

PLATES ON THE MOVE

Earth's plates move extremely slowly, at speeds of between
1 and 4 centimeters a year. As plates move apart, molten rock rises
to the surface and solidifies to form new crust. Now and again,
plates bump into one another. The force of the crash can be
powerful enough to create a new mountain range.

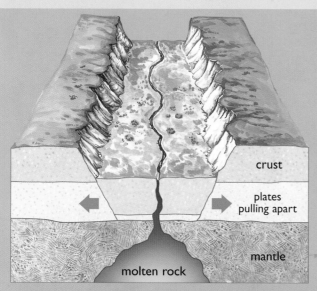

△ When plates pull apart on land, cracks appear
in the crust. Molten rock seeps up, filling the space
between the plates and forming long valleys.

△ Iceland is a country that sits on two plates which
are pulling apart. The long, deep crack between the
two plates is known as a rift valley.

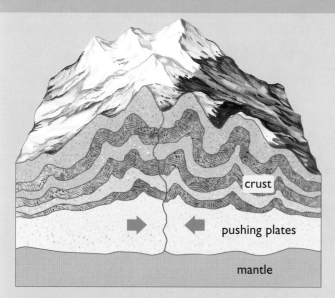

△ When two plates push together, the crust of
Earth crumples and folds. Gradually, the land
is forced up and new mountains are created.

△ The Himalayan mountains were formed by two
plates pushing together. The plates are still moving,
so the Himalayas keep growing taller!

Shifting continents

Earthquakes, volcanoes, mountains and **valleys** are not the only evidence we have of the Earth's restless nature. Gradually, over many millions of years, the movement of the **plates** changes the position of the **continents**. By looking at how the continents have moved in the past, we can predict what might happen to them in the future.

▷ This diagram shows how our world looked in the past, what it is like today and how it might look in the future.

TODAY

Today, there are seven continents separated by several oceans and many seas. Land near the North and South Poles is very cold, while land near the **equator** is warm. There is a huge variety of plant and animal life in this world, including humans.

PRESENT ◁ ◁ ◁

FUTURE ▷ ▷ ▷

5 MILLION YEARS

Five million years in the future, scientists predict that the continents will have moved a little more, bringing Europe and Africa closer together. At this time, the world is much colder, with ice covering many regions. Humans have died out, but other animals have survived and **adapted** to the cold.

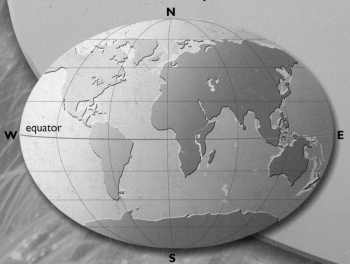

100 MILLION YEARS

One hundred million years in the future, the continents look very different to how they do today. The world has warmed up, causing the ice to melt and the sea level to go up. The warm, wet weather has given rise to a wide variety of amazing animal life.

PAST ▷▷▷

200 MILLION YEARS AGO

Scientists believe that, 200 million years ago, most of the land on Earth fitted together in one huge continent known as Pangaea. At the time of Pangaea, the world was warm and wet. Dinosaurs roamed the land.

120 MILLION YEARS AGO

By 120 million years ago, the **plates** had broken apart, creating separate, smaller continents. Different kinds of plants and animals **evolved** separately in different parts of the world.

200 MILLION YEARS

Two hundred million years in the future, Earth has come full circle. The continents have joined up again to form one huge continent, surrounded by a vast ocean. We have called this continent Pangaea II. This is a world of extremes. It is cold and windy at the coast, but hot and dry inland, yet life still survives.

Our world today

Our world is divided into seven **continents**, which are surrounded by oceans. There are different patterns of weather, or **climates**, around the world. Near the **equator**, which is an imaginary line running around the middle of Earth, it is always hot. Near the **poles**, it is always cold. The places in between have a temperate climate, which is neither too hot nor too cold. Different regions have their own landscape, plants and animals, depending on their climate.

▽ Marked on this world map are all the continents and oceans. You can also see areas, such as the Mediterranean Sea, the Amazon Basin and the Bay of Bengal, which appear later in the book.

MAP KEY

Below you will find the different landscapes that appear on our world map.

- ocean
- desert
- grassland
- ice and tundra
- coral reef
- mountains
- rainforest
- deciduous forest
- evergreen forest
- swamp and marsh

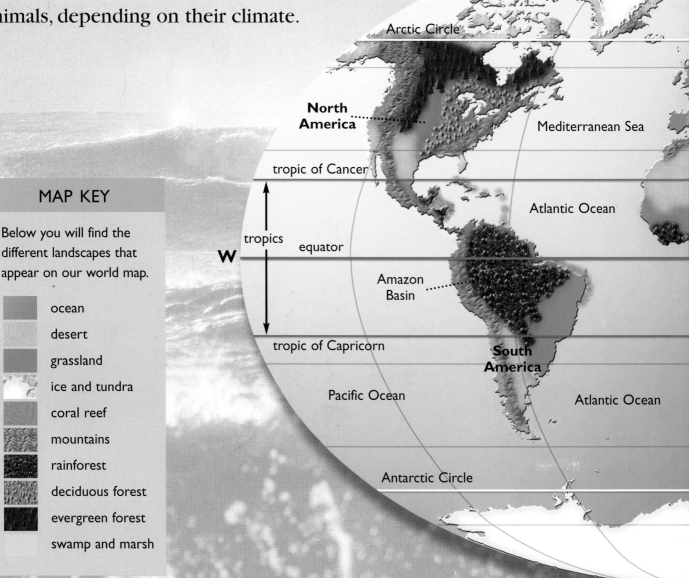

Arctic Ocean

Arctic Circle

North America

tropic of Cancer

Mediterranean Sea

Atlantic Ocean

tropics

W

equator

Amazon Basin

tropic of Capricorn

South America

Pacific Ocean

Atlantic Ocean

Antarctic Circle

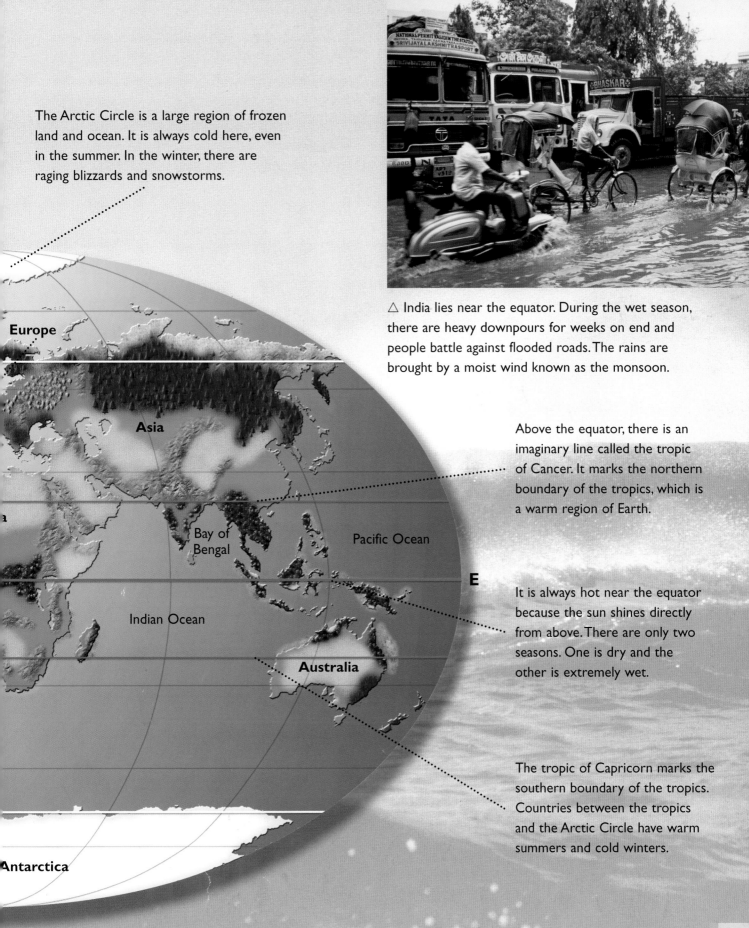

The Arctic Circle is a large region of frozen land and ocean. It is always cold here, even in the summer. In the winter, there are raging blizzards and snowstorms.

Europe

Asia

Bay of Bengal

Pacific Ocean

Indian Ocean

Australia

E

Antarctica

△ India lies near the equator. During the wet season, there are heavy downpours for weeks on end and people battle against flooded roads. The rains are brought by a moist wind known as the monsoon.

Above the equator, there is an imaginary line called the tropic of Cancer. It marks the northern boundary of the tropics, which is a warm region of Earth.

It is always hot near the equator because the sun shines directly from above. There are only two seasons. One is dry and the other is extremely wet.

The tropic of Capricorn marks the southern boundary of the tropics. Countries between the tropics and the Arctic Circle have warm summers and cold winters.

9

Earth's habitats

A **habitat** is an environment in which an animal makes its home. On Earth today, there is a wide variety of habitats, ranging from burning hot deserts to freezing-cold, icy lands. All the animals that live in a habitat are suited to it. A walrus has a thick layer of fat to protect itself from the cold, while a camel has a hump to store water in the dry desert. In this book, our panel of scientists has tried to imagine how these habitats might change in the future.

In many cases, conditions in our future worlds are more extreme than they are now. Deserts are hotter and drier, mountains are higher and forests are thicker. Even so, these extreme habitats share the same features as habitats found on Earth today.

The animals in this book also have a lot in common with animals of today. We know that, even in extreme conditions, animals will find similar ways to **adapt** and survive, just as they have done for millions of years.

RAINFOREST

△ Thick, green rainforests are home to a huge variety of animals, such as this iguana. Rainforests only grow where it is warm and wet all year.

CONIFEROUS FOREST

△ Coniferous forest trees, such as pines and firs, keep their leaves all year round. Animals, such as moose, live here.

ICE AND TUNDRA

△ These musk oxen live on a flat, treeless land called the **tundra**. The tundra lies at the edge of a thick sheet of ice that covers the North **Pole**.

SWAMP

△ Swamps are areas of land submerged beneath shallow water. They provide a **fertile** home to many plants and animals, including this heron.

DESERT

△ Deserts, such as the Sahara in North Africa, are dry, inhospitable habitats. Only the most hardy animals, such as camels or lizards, can survive here.

OCEAN

△ Today, four great oceans and many smaller seas cover more than two thirds of the planet's surface. They are full of life, such as this giant whale.

CORAL REEF

△ Coral reefs are living **organisms** made up of millions of tiny creatures. They are often described as colorful underwater gardens.

MOUNTAIN

△ A bird of prey soars above jagged mountains. These peaks are topped with ice and snow all year round. Few plants grow on the tallest mountains.

DECIDUOUS WOODLAND

△ Deciduous forests are full of trees, such as oaks and birches, that shed their leaves in autumn. Cool-climate animals, such as deer, live here.

GRASSLAND

△ Grassland includes pampas, flat plains, prairie, tropical savannah and farmland. Herds of elephants roam across the African savannah in this picture.

The animal kingdom

Earth today is teeming with life. There are millions of different kinds of animals. To make animals easier to study, scientists have split them into groups. There are two main divisions: vertebrates and invertebrates. Vertebrates are animals with backbones and invertebrates are animals that do not have a backbone. Within each division, there are more groups. Vertebrate animals include fish, birds and large **mammals** such as lions and elephants. Humans are vertebrates.

Invertebrates are a huge group. They include lots of small creatures, including snails, worms, crabs and jellyfish, and **insects** such as bees, butterflies and beetles. Many invertebrates live in the ocean.

All of the future animals in this book fit into these groups and share their basic characteristics. The creatures we have imagined are **descendants** of present-day animals. In many cases, they look a bit like their **ancestors** and behave in similar ways.

▷ Here you can see a few examples of vertebrate and invertebrate animals. As there are so many invertebrates in our world today, we have chosen examples of animals whose imaginary descendants appear later on in the book.

VERTEBRATES

- All vertebrates have a backbone.
- They have a skeleton made of bone or cartilage.
- They never have more than four limbs.

MAMMALS	BIRDS	REPTILES	AMPHIBIANS	FISH

Warm-blooded animals that give birth to live young. Most mammals are hairy but a few, such as whales, are not. Humans and bats are mammals.	Warm-blooded animals with feathers and wings whose young hatch from eggs. Most birds can fly but a few, such as penguins and ostriches, cannot.	Cold-blooded animals with dry, scaly skin which live in warm **climates**. Most **reptiles** lay eggs but a few give birth to live young. Lizards are reptiles.	Cold-blooded animals that spend part of their lives in water and part on land. They include frogs, toads and newts. They have very moist skin.	Cold-blooded animals that live in water. Most have fins and a tail which they use for swimming. Their young usually hatch from eggs. Cod and sharks are fish.

Cold- or warm-blooded?

Animals can be classified according to the temperature of their bodies. Warm-blooded animals keep the same body temperature whatever the weather is like outside. Cold-blooded animals are different. Their body temperature changes depending on how cold or warm it is around them. All invertebrate animals are cold-blooded.

▷ A crocodile is a cold-blooded reptile. When it lies in the sun, its body warms up. In cold water, it cools down.

INVERTEBRATES

- Invertebrates have no backbone and no skeleton inside their bodies.
- They have soft bodies but some have a hard outer covering, called an exoskeleton, as well.

MOLLUSCS

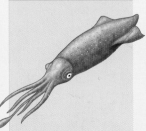

These are animals with soft bodies that often live in water. Many molluscs have a shell to protect their bodies.

ARTHROPODS

These are small animals with jointed legs, bodies made up of sections and a hard covering outside their bodies.

CEPHALOPODS

GASTROPODS

CEPHALOPODS
This group includes octopuses and squids. These creatures all live in the ocean. Squids and octopuses have eight arms. Squids also have two long tentacles.

GASTROPODS
This group includes snails and slugs. Snails crawl along using the muscular 'foot' under their bellies. They have a single coiled shell on top of their soft bodies.

INSECTS

ARACHNIDS

INSECTS
These have six legs and three body parts. Bees, butterflies and beetles are all insects. Most insects have wings and can fly. A few, such as large beetles, cannot fly.

ARACHNIDS
Arachnids have eight legs and two body parts. Unlike insects, they have no wings. They include spiders, scorpions and mites. All spiders spin silk and many make webs.

Understanding evolution

To predict what might happen to life on Earth in the future, we first need to look at the past. Over millions of years, animals have gradually **evolved**, or changed, to suit their environment. This slow process is called evolution. All the animals around us are unique. Each time one is born, it is slightly different to its parents. It takes many thousands of years for these differences to become noticeable.

▽ This herd of zebras may look alike but there are differences. Just as humans all have different swirling patterns on their fingerprints, each zebra has its own particular set of stripes. No two coats are the same.

CHANGE OF HABIT

Sometimes an animal gradually alters its behaviour to suit its surroundings. Scientists believe that this is why the kiwi, a small flightless bird from New Zealand, gave up using its wings. Kiwis live in burrows, feeding on worms, **insects** and berries. Their habits are so like those of **mammals** that they are sometimes called 'honorary mammals'.

Scientists believe that kiwis stopped flying because there were no **predators** on the ground to hunt them down. The kiwis were safe and didn't need to fly off to escape. Slowly, they evolved into ground-loving creatures. It was only when humans introduced predators, such as rats, cats and dogs, to New Zealand that the kiwis came under threat.

Filling a niche

Every animal fits into a **niche**. The home it lives in, the food it eats, and everything it does in its daily life forms its niche. Every so often, a new niche, or gap, becomes free. When kiwis arrived in New Zealand, they found a free niche. They gave up flying to live on the ground, and eat fruit and insects. In other places, this niche is filled by small mammals, such as hedgehogs.

All about body shape

One of the most noticeable changes in evolution is a change in body shape. Animals' bodies slowly **adapt** to make the most of their surroundings. Seals, dolphins, penguins and many fish have streamlined bodies to suit life in the water. Their long, smooth shape helps them to speed through the ocean.

Birds, which usually spend their lives in the air, have different wing shapes to suit their own particular style of flying.

Some birds have short, broad wings for darting about. Others have long, narrow wings for gliding and soaring over long distances. But birds are not the only animals to evolve a body shape that is ideally suited to flying. Bats also fly. Although bats and birds come from very different **ancestors**, their wings share the same basic, aerodynamic design. Humans even copied this design from nature when they invented the airplane!

▷ Living in a crowded **habitat**, such as a forest, can make flight difficult. The short, broad wings of this blue tit are perfect for twisting and turning as it darts from branch to branch, snapping up small insects as it goes.

▽ This shark's torpedo-shaped body and fins help it to cut through the water at top speed. A thrust of its tail fin propels it through the water to snatch **prey**, while the dorsal fin on its back acts as a stabilizer to stop it rolling from side to side in the water.

△ The long, narrow wings of this albatross are perfect for fast gliding in wide open spaces. By using winds cleverly, it keeps airborne for most of the time without having to flap its wings.

A fight for survival

The way animals change and **adapt** to suit their surroundings is just one part of evolution. There are many other obstacles to overcome in the struggle for survival. Animals must compete with other animals for space to live in and food to eat. They must defend themselves against **predators** and protect their young so that they can grow into adults.

They must cope with terrible diseases and extreme weather conditions. Only animals that are best equipped to overcome these difficulties survive. Sometimes, whole **species** of animals cannot adapt and become **extinct**, which means that they die out completely. Below, you can find out about some of the strategies animals use to ensure their survival.

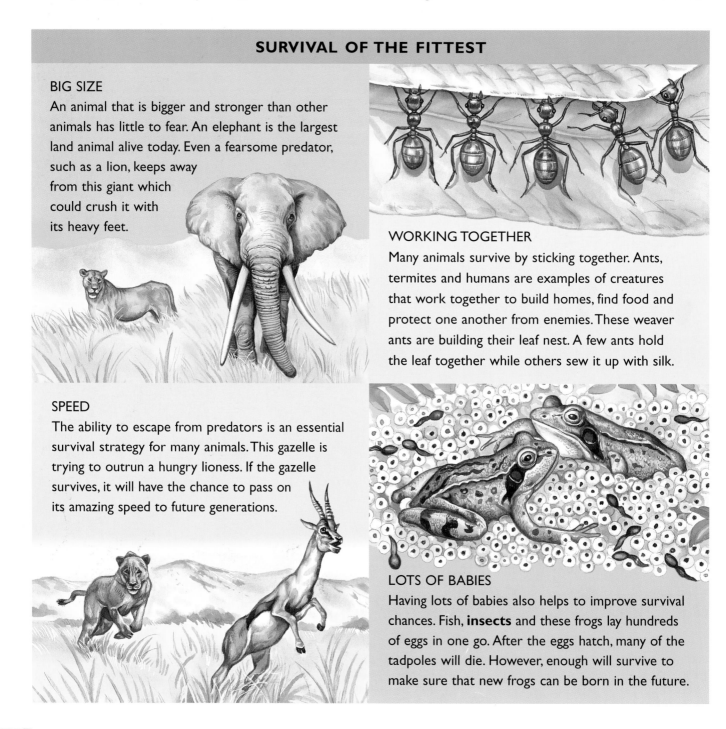

SURVIVAL OF THE FITTEST

BIG SIZE
An animal that is bigger and stronger than other animals has little to fear. An elephant is the largest land animal alive today. Even a fearsome predator, such as a lion, keeps away from this giant which could crush it with its heavy feet.

WORKING TOGETHER
Many animals survive by sticking together. Ants, termites and humans are examples of creatures that work together to build homes, find food and protect one another from enemies. These weaver ants are building their leaf nest. A few ants hold the leaf together while others sew it up with silk.

SPEED
The ability to escape from predators is an essential survival strategy for many animals. This gazelle is trying to outrun a hungry lioness. If the gazelle survives, it will have the chance to pass on its amazing speed to future generations.

LOTS OF BABIES
Having lots of babies also helps to improve survival chances. Fish, **insects** and these frogs lay hundreds of eggs in one go. After the eggs hatch, many of the tadpoles will die. However, enough will survive to make sure that new frogs can be born in the future.

HOW DOES A NEW SPECIES DEVELOP?

All animals can be divided into different species. Animals of the same species share similar characteristics and can breed with one another. One example of how new species **evolve** can be found in a group of birds, called finches. Fourteen different species of finch live on the Galápagos Islands in South America. Scientists believe that they are all **descendants** of the same **ancestor**.

1 Millions of years ago, a small group of finches from South America was blown far off course towards a cluster of islands called the Galápagos Islands.

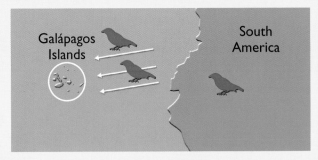

△ The cactus finch is one species of finch that lives on the Galápagos Islands. It has a long, sharp, narrow beak. It feeds on the prickly pear cactus, using its beak to pierce the thick, tough skin of the cactus fruit to reach the soft, juicy flesh underneath.

2 The finches landed on two different islands. There were now two separate groups, which were cut off from the mainland and from each other. Each group began to breed among itself.

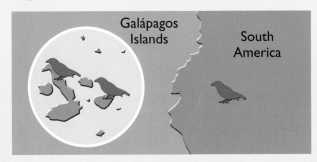

3 Over thousands of years, the two groups of finches adapted to the different **habitats** on their islands and slowly evolved into separate species.

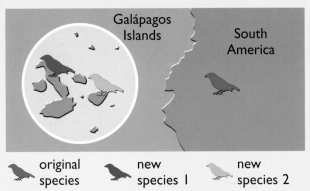

original species   new species 1   new species 2

△ The woodpecker finch is a completely different species to the cactus finch. It is one of the few birds in the world to use a tool to help it feed. It prys insects with a cactus spine from small holes in trees.

Clues from the past

One of the best ways for scientists to unlock the secrets of evolution is by studying clues from the past. When an animal or plant dies, it often leaves its impression or remains behind in rock. This is a **fossil**. Scientists study fossils to find out about animals that lived in the past, and when and where they lived.

Usually, only the bones or shell of an animal turn into fossils. It is unusual for the brain or other **organs** to be preserved. This makes it difficult to find out what an animal looked like, what it ate or how it behaved. So scientists look for other clues. A tooth can tell us if an animal ate meat or plants. Fossilized tracks, or footprints, can tell us a lot about the size or speed of an animal. These clues help scientists piece together the story of life on Earth.

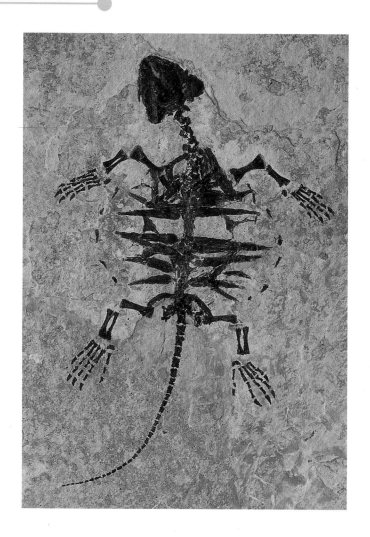

▷ This turtle fossil was found in the USA. Scientists can work out the age of a fossil by studying the layers of rock around it. Scientists believe that this turtle lived around 50 million years ago.

LIFE ON EARTH

Scientists estimate that Earth is about 4.5 billion years old. The first life appeared in the oceans, between 3 and 4 billion years ago. At first, there were only simple **organisms** without backbones. Much later, vertebrates, which are animals with backbones, appeared and life began to move from the ocean on to land. Humans have only been around for a short while. In this panel, you can trace the story of life on Earth from the past to the present. You can read about how life might **evolve** in the future later in the book.

1,000 MILLION YEARS AGO

The first animals had soft bodies and lived in the oceans. They evolved from simple creatures called bacteria. Jellyfish and worms all lived at this time.

500 MILLION YEARS AGO

The first fish appeared about 500 million years ago. Then, 370 million years ago, other fish-like creatures began to breathe air, developed legs and moved to the land.

HOW A FOSSIL IS FORMED

When an animal dies and sinks to the bottom of a river, swamp or ocean, the soft parts of its body rot away, leaving only the bones behind. Layers of mud and sand cover the bones. Over millions of years, the mud and sand harden and turn to stone. Slowly, the bones also turn to stone. Much later, and only occasionally, the fossil is exposed when the layers of rock above it are worn away.

Modern techniques

Recently, scientists have discovered that the story of every animal's evolution is hidden inside its genes. Genes are sets of information which determine the way animals behave or what they look like. This information is passed from one generation to the next. For example, if parents have freckles and green eyes, then their children may inherit the same features.

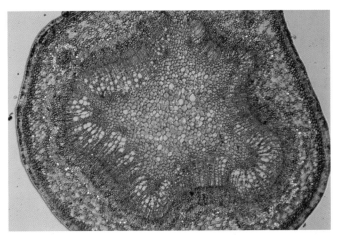

△ All living things are made up of tiny **cells**. This picture shows one cell viewed through a powerful microscope.

240 MILLION YEARS AGO
This was the age of the dinosaurs. Other **reptiles**, such as crocodiles, also appeared at this time. Around 65 million years ago, a mysterious event wiped out all dinosaurs.

65 MILLION YEARS AGO
After dinosaurs died out, **mammals** flourished and some grew to huge sizes. Flying reptiles, which became the first birds, ruled the skies. Flowering plants and **insects** also thrived.

2 MILLION YEARS AGO TO TODAY
The **ancestors** of humans first appeared around 2 million years ago. Later, they began to use tools. Today, humans have built big cities and dominate the planet.

Imagining the future

Can you predict which animals might live in the future and what they might look like? It's not as difficult as it sounds. In this book, we have tried to imagine how the world's **climates** and **habitats** might change and how animals might **adapt**. Now it's your turn! Choose an animal that is alive today, pick a time period and one of the future habitats from the book. Then ask a few scientific questions to see how your animal will **evolve**.

◁ Professor Neill Alexander is a leading biologist. He helped to design many of the creatures in this book, including the desert hopper on the opposite page.

"Be bold when you imagine the animals of the future. Evolution has done amazing things in the past and is likely to be just as amazing in the future. But make sure your creatures have what it takes to survive in a harsh world."

Inventing your own creature

Check out the hints and tips on these pages, then design your own future critter! Try picking animals from different groups. You could choose a **mammal**, such as a bear, or a **reptile**, such as a snake. Picture the habitat it might live in and how it might adapt to survive. It's a good idea to make different drawings of your creature. Think about how it moves, its size and what features it has. Does it have legs, tentacles or feelers? Finally, don't forget to give your creature a name!

TOP ANIMAL EVOLUTION TIPS

Here are a few evolutionary tips to think about while you are inventing your creature.

- The ability to live in different habitats gives animals a good chance of survival.
- Animals that live in the cold may develop fat or fur for insulation.
- Animals living in deserts have to find ways to store water.
- A varied diet is useful when food becomes scarce.
- Growing in size helps to protect an animal from **predators**.
- Animals have moved from the ocean to the land in Earth's history.

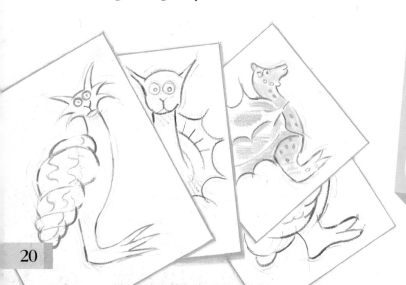

HOW DOES A SNAIL BECOME A DESERT HOPPER?

One of the strange creatures you'll find in the pages of this book is the desert hopper, a giant snail that hops! The creature we created lives in a hot, dry desert called the Rainshadow Desert. So what questions did we ask to work out how a small slimy snail could evolve into a huge hopping snail? Read on to find out!

1 WHICH MODERN-DAY ANIMAL IS OUR STARTING POINT?

There are more than 80,000 kinds of snail alive today. Snails share several characteristics. They move around on a muscular foot, sliding along on a trail of slime. They all have a hard shell to protect their soft bodies. There is one type of snail that hops. It lives in the ocean and uses its foot to escape from predators.

2 WHAT ARE ITS CHANCES OF SURVIVAL IN A NEW ENVIRONMENT?

Snails are very adaptable. They live all over the world, from back gardens to mountains and oceans. They can even live in deserts. Although snails need to keep moist, they can survive in dry conditions by sealing themselves inside their shells with a door of dried slime. They are also not fussy eaters. They feed on both plants and animals.

3 HOW COULD IT ADAPT AND EVOLVE?

Two hundred million years in the future, the snail has to cope with the extreme environment of the Rainshadow Desert. The desert is bone dry, so it is important to conserve water. Food is scarce too. The snail has evolved so that it no longer gives off a slime trail. This way, valuable moisture stays inside its body. Instead of crawling, it now hops. Hopping allows the snail to travel longer distances in search of food.

4 WHAT DOES THE NEW CREATURE LOOK LIKE?

The desert hopper is much larger than its **ancestors**. It is 12 inches (30 centimeters) tall and 8 inches (20 centimeters) long, which is about the size of a rabbit. It has been able to grow bigger because there are few creatures around to compete with for food.

Its skin is tough and scaly, more like the skin of a reptile than a snail. The tough skin helps to stop moisture escaping from the desert hopper's body.

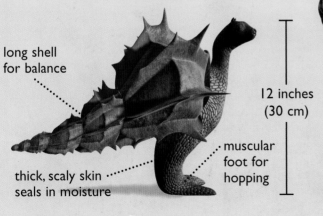

long shell for balance

12 inches (30 cm)

thick, scaly skin seals in moisture

muscular foot for hopping

5 MILLION YEARS

Five million years in the future, a great Ice Age has descended on Earth. The icecaps which covered the North and South **Poles** in human times now stretch down towards the **equator**. Earth is a cold, dry place. Many animals have become **extinct**, including humans. Only the most adaptable creatures have been able adjust to the extreme conditions of this future world.

▽ This map shows what our world might look like in 5 million years.

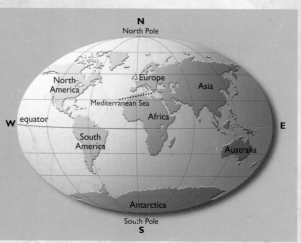

W   equator

HUMAN TIMES

THE FUTURE

North American Desert

In human times, North America was a rich, **fertile** continent. Five million years in the future, the green fields have dried up, leaving a cold, dry desert.

Earth in human times

Even in human times, the North and South Poles were the coldest places on the planet. But although many countries were cold, countries close to the equator were hot and humid. This range of temperatures meant that many different **species evolved** to suit the different living conditions.

N
North Pole

North America   Europe   Asia

Mediterranean Sea

W   equator   Africa   E

South America

Australia

Antarctica

South Pole
S

MAP KEY

land areas

grassland

mountains

desert

salt flats

icecaps

ocean

North European Ice

In human times, Northern Europe was known for its bustling towns and productive farmlands. Five million years in the future, it is the coldest region on the planet. The land is treeless and covered in snow. The oceans are icy cold.

HUMAN TIMES

THE FUTURE

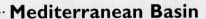

E

Mediterranean Basin

In human times, the Mediterranean coast was full of busy, holiday resorts. Five million years in the future, the Mediterranean Sea has dried up, leaving a crust of white salt.

HUMAN TIMES

THE FUTURE

HUMAN TIMES

THE FUTURE

Amazon Grasslands

In human times, the Amazon was home to a hot, humid rainforest. Five million years in the future, the tall trees have been replaced by dry grasslands.

North European Ice

The Ice Age has turned Northern Europe into a cold, desolate place. Many countries are completely covered by a thick layer of ice. **Glaciers**, which are great rivers of ice, creep slowly down **valleys** towards the sea. Huge icebergs float in the freezing waters of the ocean. It is hard to imagine how life can survive in these frozen lands.

Gannetwhale

One animal that has **adapted** perfectly to the icy water is the gannetwhale, a large underwater hunter. Gannetwhales have taken the place of sea **mammals**, such as sea lions, seals and walruses, which could not survive in the freezing temperatures of the Ice Age.

However, gannetwhales are not mammals. They are giant birds! These creatures spend most of their lives in the ocean, speeding through the water and catching fish with their long narrow beaks.

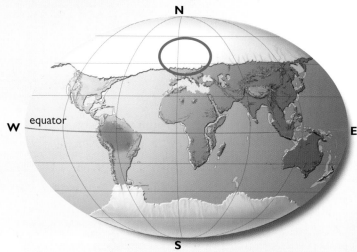

△ At the edge of the thick sheet of ice that covers Northern Europe, the sea and land are bitterly cold.

▽ In the summertime, female gannnetwhales find a nesting ground where they lay their eggs and keep them warm until they hatch. Gannetwhales are fast and agile underwater but on land, they move with difficulty. Both the mothers and their eggs are at risk from **predators**.

Laying eggs

The summer is short in Northern Europe, so the gannetwhales must act quickly to lay their eggs and raise their young while temperatures are slightly warmer. Each female gannetwhale lays one egg, tucking it under her tail where it can benefit from the warmth of her belly. She guards the egg ferociously until it hatches, snapping her beak at any predator that dares to come near. While the mothers wait for their eggs to hatch, males hunt for food in the ocean, bringing back food for their families.

EVOLUTION IN ACTION

In many ways, gannetwhales look like the penguins that swam in the cold oceans of our world. Like the penguin, the gannetwhale has adapted perfectly to its environment. Its wings have **evolved** into flippers to help it speed through the water and it has developed a thick layer of fat to keep it warm in the icy water.

△ The torpedo-shaped body and strong flippers of a penguin make it a fast, graceful swimmer.

Surviving in a cold climate

At the edge of the ice mountains and **glaciers** of Northern Europe, there is a wide belt of **tundra** stretching as far as the eye can see. The tundra is a flat, treeless land. Only a few small bushes and tough plants grow on the ground. Just below the surface, the soil is frozen solid. Food is extremely hard to find on the tundra and the animals that live here must cope with temperatures below freezing point all year round.

The snowstalker is one creature that has developed excellent defenses against the cold. It has a thick, shaggy coat to keep its body warm and white fur to **camouflage** it against the snow and ice.

▷ Snowstalkers are fearsome hunters. They attack swiftly and silently, pinning down their victims with their sharp claws and biting them with their long, pointed teeth.

Snowstalkers hunt alone, padding silently across the snow on their broad, flat feet. Although snowstalkers are not particularly big, they are deadly hunters. They can kill animals that are much larger than themselves by sinking their long teeth into their victim's throat.

Snowstalker's family life

Female snowstalkers have their babies at the start of the short summer to give them the chance to grow while the weather is warmer. Life is tough for the youngsters and they spend much of their time alone while their mother is away hunting for food.

▽ Baby snowstalkers play tug-of-war with a scrap of meat. Playfighting strengthens the youngsters' jaws. It also teaches them important skills for later life, when they must go it alone in the snow and ice.

Shagrat

Snowstalkers hunt for their favourite food, which is shagrats. Large herds of shagrats roam the tundra, grazing on the short grass. They are **rodents**, which are a type of small **mammal**. But shagrats are much bigger than their **ancestors**. Like many animals that live in cold regions, they have **evolved** large bodies to protect them from the bitter cold. This is because large bodies hold in heat better than small bodies.

▷ A herd of shagrats trudges across the snow. It is vital that they stick together. A large group has more chance of fighting off a **predator**, such as a hungry snowstalker.

27

The Mediterranean Basin

Picture the Mediterranean coast in human times. It was one of the world's busiest holiday destinations. All year round, crowds of people visited the beaches to soak up the sun, sea and sand.

Now imagine a dazzling-white salt lake, baked dry by the scorching sun. This is the Mediterranean region of the future. To survive on the salt flats, animals must **adapt** to the cool, dry **climate** and harsh living conditions.

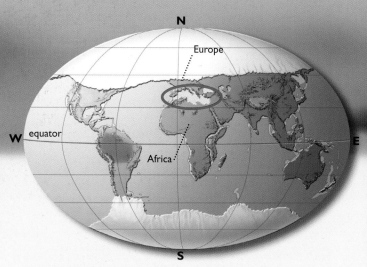

△ The Mediterranean Basin lies between the **continents** of Europe and Africa.

Cryptile lizard

Reptiles, such as snakes and lizards, have always survived well in dry climates, so it is no surprise to find that the most successful creature here is a lizard called the cryptile lizard. Around the edges of the salt flats, swarms of black flies gather. These tiny flies give the cryptile lizard all the food it needs. It catches the flies in the frill of skin around its neck, which acts as a sticky net. As it runs through a cloud of flies, they stick to the net as if to flypaper. The cryptile quickly plucks off the **insects** with its long tongue.

Changing color

The cryptile lizard is a master of disguise. Its pale color allows it to fade into the white salt background. But it does not always choose to go unnoticed. When it wants to find a mate, it spreads its neck frill wide and floods it with bright colors. This display makes it stand out against the salt so that it can be seen by females from miles around.

△ The Mediterranean Basin is a huge expanse of shimmering salt, surrounded by rocky mountains. It hardly ever rains here, but when it does, the surface of the salt flats turns into a salty mush.

▽ The cryptile lizard flicks out its long tongue into a cloud of flies. The water on the salt flats is too salty to drink, so the flies provide the cryptile with moisture as well as food.

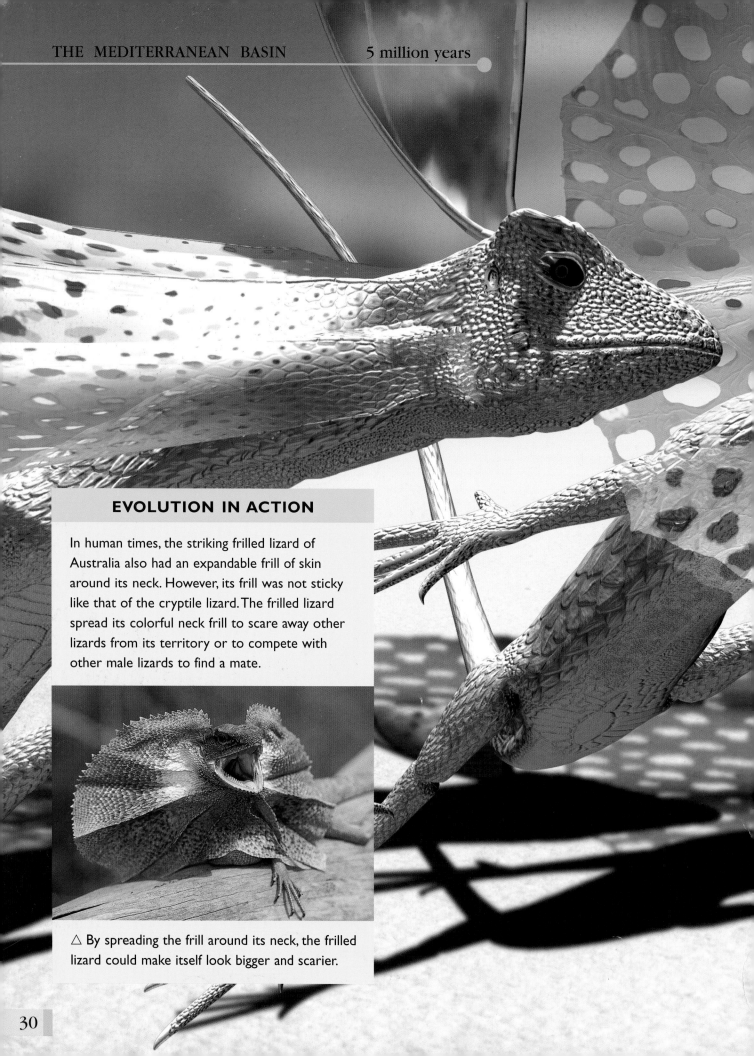

EVOLUTION IN ACTION

In human times, the striking frilled lizard of Australia also had an expandable frill of skin around its neck. However, its frill was not sticky like that of the cryptile lizard. The frilled lizard spread its colorful neck frill to scare away other lizards from its territory or to compete with other male lizards to find a mate.

△ By spreading the frill around its neck, the frilled lizard could make itself look bigger and scarier.

△ When a female cryptile spots the multi-colored display of the male cryptile, she races across the salt flats to meet her new mate. The pair then run across the salt together, in a strange mating ritual.

Life in the karst

Around the shores of the salt flats, there is a dry, grey and rocky region called a karst. It is formed from limestone, which is a type of rock that easily soaks up water. Over millions of years, water has gradually worn away the rock, leaving deep cracks, known as grykes.

Different kinds of creatures make their home on the karst to those on the salt flats. Some **mammals** and **insects** live down in the grykes, where they are protected from the cold wind. Other animals spend their time on the rocky surface, sniffing around for scraps of food scattered among the rocks.

Scrofa

Animals that live on the karst must **adapt** to the rocky ground, and scrofas have adapted perfectly. They are lightly-built creatures with slim, flexible legs and delicate hooves. This allows them to bound along the uneven surface, easily leaping over any deep grykes that lie in their way.

Scrofas spend most of the day foraging for food, sniffing out plants and insects with their long snouts. They live in close family groups. The adults keep a protective eye on their young, called scroflets, as they skip about the karst. The grykes are full of danger.

EVOLUTION IN ACTION

The scrofas' **ancestors** were wild pigs, which were common in human times. Wild pigs could live in almost any environment and eat any kind of food. When the Ice Age came and food became hard to find, other creatures died out. But pig-like creatures survived thanks to their ability to eat a variety of foods and to live in cold **climates**.

◁ Wild pigs were **omnivores**, which means that they ate both meat and plants. Their diet consisted of small animals, roots and grains.

Gryken

Deep in the grykes, another mammal is lying in wait for the scroflets. It is a slinky **predator** called a gryken and it is well adapted to life in this rocky land. Its long, supple body is perfect for weaving through the twists and turns of the grykes. Black and white stripes on its head disguise its eyes against the layers of rock. If a baby scroflet becomes separated from the rest of the herd, the gryken will strike, dragging its victim down into the deep cracks.

△ A gryken pokes its head out of the rocks, sniffing the air for food. Its long, sharp teeth help it to puncture the thick skins of scroflets.

▽ A mother scrofa chases a gryken down into the grykes. Behind her, the young scroflets are safe to continue searching for food.

33

The Amazon Grasslands

When humans lived on Earth, the Amazon was known for its warm, wet rainforest and mighty Amazon river. Five million years later, the weather is colder and drier. The trees have disappeared and the Amazon river has been reduced to smaller rivers and streams. All that remains is dry grassland, which is frequently burned back by violent bushfires.

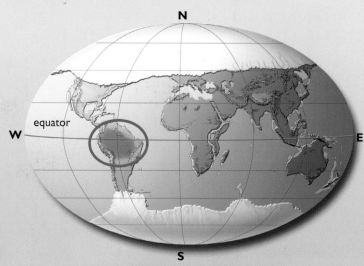

△ The Amazon Grasslands lie at the tip of what was once the **continent** of South America.

Babookaris

To survive the change from forest to grasslands, animals had to move down from the trees and **adapt** to life on the ground. One creature from this future world that is perfectly adapted to living on the ground is a monkey, called the babookari. Large troupes of babookaris make their home in the grasslands, eating fish, insects and plants.

▷ Babookaris signal to one another by waving their long, straight tails. This clever system of communication is just one example of the monkeys' intelligence.

The babookari's monkey **ancestors** lived in the rainforest, swinging from tree to tree with their flexible, gripping tails. With no forest to live in, babookaris use their tails for a different purpose. They stay in contact with each other by waving their tails above the grass. But, because their tails are disguised as blades of grass, they are invisible to their enemies.

Babookaris are **omnivores**, which means they eat both plants and animals. They are highly intelligent and have learned how to make traps to catch fish. With their flexible fingers, they weave large hollow baskets, leaving a hole in the front for fish to swim into. They place the baskets at the edge of a river or stream, returning later to eat the fish which have become trapped inside.

Rattleback

One of the toughest creatures of the Amazon Grasslands is a **rodent**, called the rattleback. This animal gets its name from the rattling noise it makes as it shakes the hard plates on its back. The plates act as a flameproof suit, protecting the rattleback from fire. When a bushfire blazes through the grasslands, the rattleback simply flattens itself to the ground. The flames sweep overhead and the rattleback is unharmed.

△ The hard plates on the rattleback's back are made of stiff, hardened hair. They are a bit like the quills of a porcupine or a rhino's sharp horn.

Carakiller

The fastest, deadliest hunter of the Amazon Grasslands is a large bird called the carakiller. Like emus or ostriches of human times, the carakiller cannot fly. It does not need to. There is plenty of food on the ground and the carakiller is a high-speed runner.

The carakiller is a bird of prey, which means that it kills and eats meat. Apart from a spray of red and black feathers on the back of its head, the carakiller's head and neck are bald. This allows it to eat without becoming sticky with blood from its food.

Bushfire barbecue

Carakillers hunt in groups, using the frequent bushfires to their advantage. As the fire races through the grasslands, the carakillers remain one step ahead, snapping up small animals, including insects, as they try to escape the flames. Other carakillers walk behind the fire, picking over the barbecued bodies of animals that did not manage to escape.

△ Carakillers race ahead of a bushfire on their long, powerful legs. Their wings are short and stubby, and are no use for flying. Instead, carakillers use their short wings to balance their bodies as they run along.

▽ A mother guards her eggs. When they are angry, carakillers raise their red and black head feathers in a ferocious display. The feathers are also used to signal to other birds above the tall grass.

The North American Desert

In human times, North America was full of big cities, leafy forests and rich green farmlands. In this future world, the freezing temperatures of the Ice Age have turned most of the **continent** into a bitterly-cold, rocky desert. The violent **tornadoes** and sandstorms that whip across the desert make it difficult for plants to grow. Animals that live here must be able to survive for long periods of time without any food.

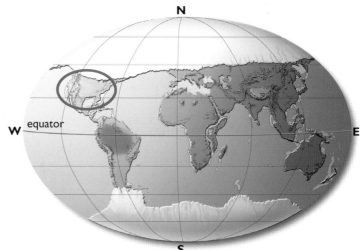

△ The North American Desert stretches across what was once the United States of America.

Deathgleaner

High above the desert, strange black creatures circle in the sky. They are deathgleaners, which are giant meat-eating bats. With their excellent eyesight and sharp sense of smell, these creatures can find food wherever it hides. Deathgleaners live in caves, huddling together during the freezing desert night. When food is hard to find, they fall into a **torpor**, which is a kind of half-sleep. This helps them to save energy for long flights.

◁ Deathgleaners have sharp teeth and clawed feet to grip their **prey**. They balance on the ground by resting on their elbows.

EVOLUTION IN ACTION

Deathgleaners have a lot in common with vampire bats from human times. Like vampire bats, deathgleaners drink blood. Both **species** also have a system for sharing food. They collect blood in special throat pouches and share it with other bats when they return to the cave.

△ Vampire bats made two holes in an animal's skin with their teeth, then lapped up the blood.

△ The deathgleaner's wide **wingspan** allows it to fly for long distances. However, it must travel in the daytime when it can glide on the warm air that rises up from the desert.

100 MILLION YEARS

One hundred million years in the future, the planet has recovered from the terrible Ice Age. Earth's **plates** have moved, changing the shape and position of the **continents**. Temperatures are several degrees higher than they were in human times and the ice that once covered the North and South **Poles** has completely melted. This has made sea levels rise and large areas of land are flooded. In this warm, wet world, conditions are perfect for life to thrive.

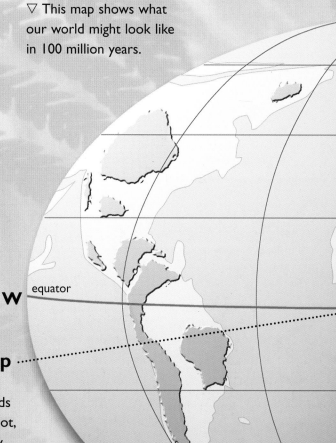

▽ This map shows what our world might look like in 100 million years.

W   equator

Bengal Swamp

The Bengal Swamp stretches for thousands of kilometers. It is a hot, damp region of murky rivers and muddy land. The swamp is **fertile** and is covered in thick green plants and trees.

Earth in human times

In human times, lots of water was frozen into the ice that covered the North and South Poles. Plenty of land was exposed so animals could move around easily. Places close to the **equator**, such as South America and Australia, had warm **climates** and **habitats**. They were similar to those we imagine, 100 million years in the future.

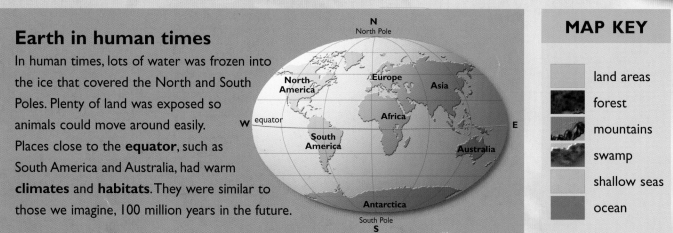

N
North Pole

North America

Europe

Asia

W   equator

Africa

E

South America

Australia

Antarctica

South Pole
S

MAP KEY

land areas

forest

mountains

swamp

shallow seas

ocean

Shallow Seas

This area is called the Shallow Seas. Many plants and animals make their home in the clear sunlit waters. There are other shallow seas around the world.

Great Plateau

The Great Plateau is a region of rocky highlands, which nestles among the peaks of the highest mountain range on Earth. At this height, the thin air makes it difficult to breathe.

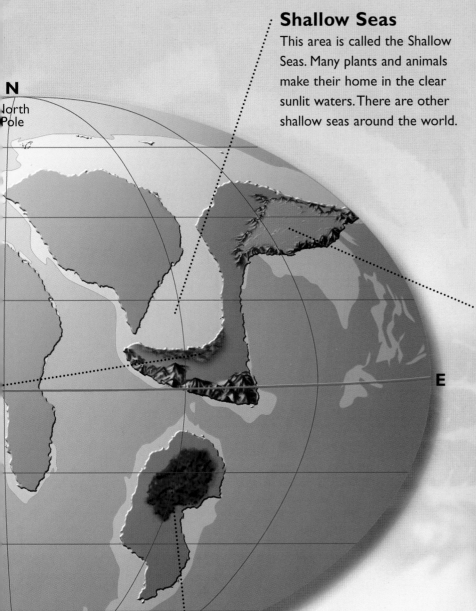

N
North Pole

E

South Pole

S

Antarctic Forest

The continent of Antarctica has moved closer to the equator and the climate is now warm and moist. A thick green rainforest covers a wide belt of land.

The Shallow Seas

In this warm world, 100 million years in the future, much more of the planet's surface is covered by water than it was in human times. An area called the Shallow Seas has formed. The water in much of the Shallow Seas is no more than 50 feet (15 meters) deep, which was the height of an average tree in human times. Sunlight reaches right down to the bottom. The warm, sunny waters are teeming with all kinds of life.

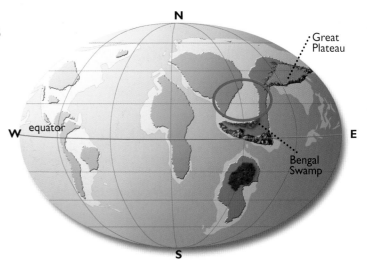

△ The Shallow Seas is a large area of shallow water that lies between the Bengal Swamp and the Great Plateau.

Rocky reefs

The floor of the Shallow Seas is covered with huge, rocky **reefs** made by plants, called **algae**. Thick red leaves grow up from the reefs. They are a good source of food for many sea creatures, while the caves and archways underneath provide a safe shelter from larger animals.

Reef glider

One animal that makes its home here is the reef glider. This teardrop-shaped creature can grow to the size of a seal from human times. On each side of its body, it has three strong, flexible paddles to push itself through the water in search of food. Young reef gliders eat algae, while adults are **carnivores** and eat meat. Fish, reef gliders breathe through **gills** which soak up **oxygen** from the water. A fish's gills are inside its body with small slits visible on the outside. A reef glider's gills trail behind its body as it swims along.

EVOLUTION IN ACTION

Reef gliders have **evolved** from sea slugs, which were small, brightly-colored, boneless animals that crawled along sea beds in human times. However, reef gliders are much bigger than sea slugs and need more food. They have paddles to allow them to swim instead of crawl. This way they can easily travel far enough to find plenty of food.

△ Like reef gliders, the sea slugs' bright colors warned **predators** that they were poisonous.

▽ Reef gliders have eyes on bendy stalks so they can see in all directions. Bumpy scent detectors on their foreheads give them an excellent sense of smell and help them to track down food in the water.

Ocean phantom

A dark shadow creeps menacingly across the surface of the **reef**. It is the huge body of an ocean phantom, the biggest **predator** in the Shallow Seas. At 33 feet (10 meters) long and 13 feet (4 meters) wide, this hunter is the size of a whale from human times. The ocean phantom acts like a giant float. On top of the float, there are sails which are filled with gas. These sails help the ocean phantom to move across the sea. Long tentacles trail in the water beneath the float.

Although the ocean phantom looks like one animal, it is actually made up of thousands of smaller creatures living together in a group called a **colony**. Each individual has **evolved** to play a particular role. The individuals may be part of the float, keeping the phantom upright or part of the sail, helping it to move. They may even be part of a tentacle dangling below to grab food. The **algae** that grow on top are plants hitching a ride with the group.

▽ The brown algae covering the phantom's body have an important role in the colony. In exchange for a safe, sunny place to live, they make **chemicals** that provide the phantom with extra food. With its field of brown algae, the ocean phantom resembles a floating farm.

On the move

Normally, the ocean phantom's sails lie flat as it drifts across the shallows. But when it goes in search of food, special chambers inside the sails fill up with gas to make the sails upright. Around the gas chambers, there is a network of tubes. By filling different tubes with water, the phantom can change the shape of its sails, allowing it to turn this way and that to catch the wind. This makes it easier to follow **prey**, such as young reef gliders feeding on the reef.

EVOLUTION IN ACTION

The Portuguese man-of-war from human times was a distant relative of the ocean phantom. Like the ocean phantom, it was made up of separate **organisms** that worked together to feed the colony. But the phantom has evolved to become much bigger than its relative. Its huge size has reduced its chances of being eaten by other animals and made it a creature to fear.

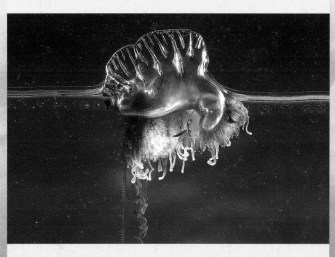

△ The Portuguese man-of-war moved using a sail. It also had tentacles to catch food.

Attack and defense

The ocean phantom glides over the sea in search of baby reef gliders for a snack. Its long tentacles have bell-shaped ends which open out and grab its victims whole. The food is then broken down into useful **chemicals** and shared out among all the individuals in the colony. Now and again, ocean phantoms are attacked. But they have a brilliant secret defense system to keep them safe from harm.

▷ This picture shows the ocean phantom's many parts and how they all work together.

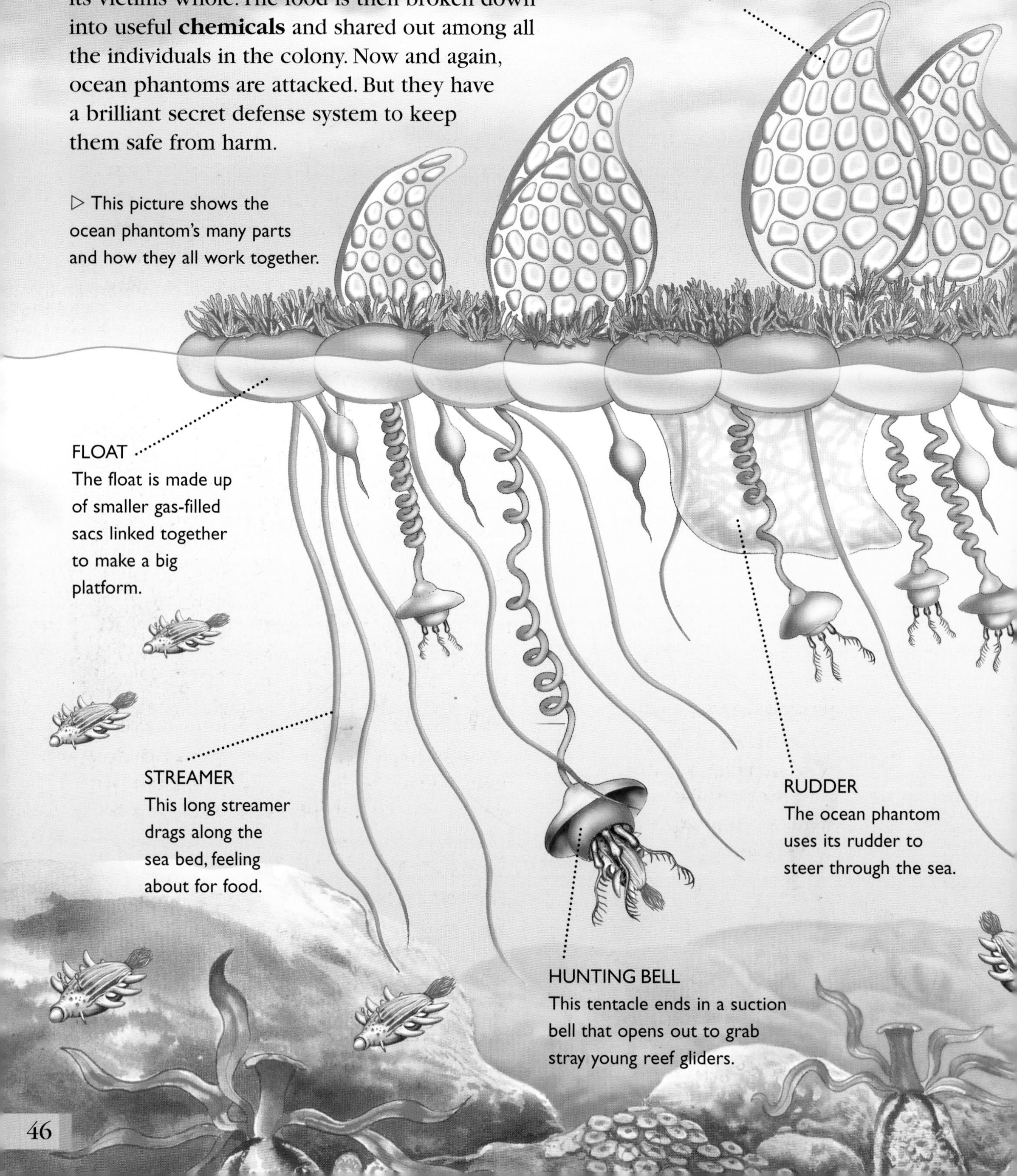

SAIL
The walls of this sail contains tubes which fill with water. The amount of water in the tubes affects the shape and position of the sail.

FLOAT
The float is made up of smaller gas-filled sacs linked together to make a big platform.

STREAMER
This long streamer drags along the sea bed, feeling about for food.

RUDDER
The ocean phantom uses its rudder to steer through the sea.

HUNTING BELL
This tentacle ends in a suction bell that opens out to grab stray young reef gliders.

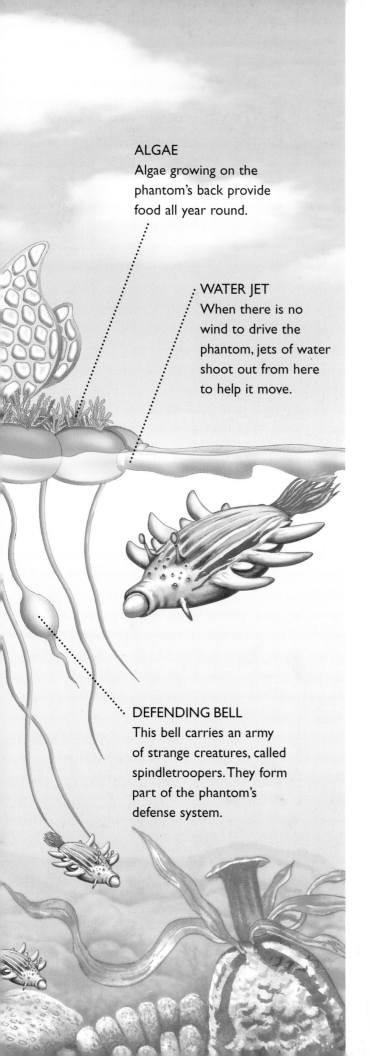

ALGAE
Algae growing on the phantom's back provide food all year round.

WATER JET
When there is no wind to drive the phantom, jets of water shoot out from here to help it move.

DEFENDING BELL
This bell carries an army of strange creatures, called spindletroopers. They form part of the phantom's defense system.

Spindletrooper surprise

Baby reef gliders are easy pickings for the ocean phantom. Fully-grown, adult reef gliders, however, are a different matter. They strike in groups, attacking from all sides and biting chunks out of the phantom's body. But the ocean phantom has a secret weapon of its own, an army of ferocious spindletroopers.

Spindletroopers **evolved** from sea spiders of human times. They live inside bells on the phantom's tentacles. When reef gliders attack, the spindletroopers fight them off. In return, the phantom provides the spindletroopers with food and a safe home. A useful partnership like this often occurs in nature. It is called a **symbiotic relationship**.

△ Spindletroopers are eight-legged fighters with sharp teeth and long claws. Although they are small, working together they can easily scare off an adult reef glider.

Born again

Sometimes, huge storms batter the Shallow Seas, whipping up heavy waves that can break an ocean phantom up into small pieces. But the phantom is still not defeated. Each piece can survive alone, slowly breeding new colony members until it forms a brand new giant ocean-going hunter.

47

The Bengal Swamp

The Bengal Swamp is a region of marshy ground covering thousands of miles. It is warm and wet all year round. The swamp runs into the sea so it contains a mixture of salt water and fresh water. Around one edge, there is a range of mountains. When it rains, soil and mud wash down from the mountains into the water, making it dark and murky. The mud at the bottom is full of **minerals**, providing plenty of **nutrients** for plants to grow.

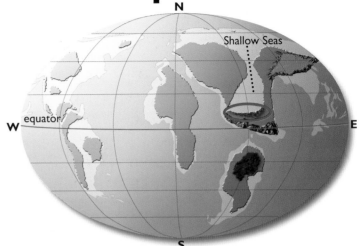

△ The Bengal Swamp lies at the edge of the Shallow Seas. Salt water from the sea flows into the swamp.

▽ Trees are dotted around the swamp. Their roots are anchored firmly in a thick bed of mud. Waterweeds and slimy **algae** cover the water's surface.

Lurkfish

The murky water makes a perfect hiding place for large hunters, such as the lurkfish. This **predator** grows up to 13 feet (4 meters) long. That's about the length of a minibus! It has lumpy, brownish skin and leafy fins which make it look like a log. This **camouflage** hides the fish from enemies, and also helps it to ambush **prey**.

The lurkfish lies in the shallows, sometimes for days on end, waiting for a victim to pass by. It barely can see through the dark water. Instead, it senses slight movements that tell it exactly where other animals are. Once a meal, such as a smaller fish, is within striking distance, the lurkfish attacks. With a sweep of its powerful tail, it darts forwards and snaps up its prey. Sometimes larger victims put up a fight, but the lurkfish has an extra trick. Special muscles along the sides of its body can deliver a super-charged electric shock. This paralyses the prey, stopping it from moving so that the lurkfish can munch its dinner in peace.

▽ The lurkfish detects its prey's movements with pointed bristles, known as barbels. The bristles cover the fish's mouth and stick up from the top of its head.

Life on the land

The rich plant life in the Bengal Swamp provides plenty of food for **herbivores**, or plant-eating animals. The biggest of these is the toraton. It is a huge **reptile**, larger than a dinosaur. An adult toraton is so huge that it has no **predators**. It spends its days peacefully chewing plants. In one day, it can eat up to 1,320 pounds (600 kilograms) of leaves. That's three times more than a rhinoceros ate in human times. Like other reptiles, toratons lay eggs. Their shells are so tough that the mothers have to bite them open to help the babies hatch. Toratons look after their young for five years, until they reach the size of a baby elephant.

A GIANT BEAST

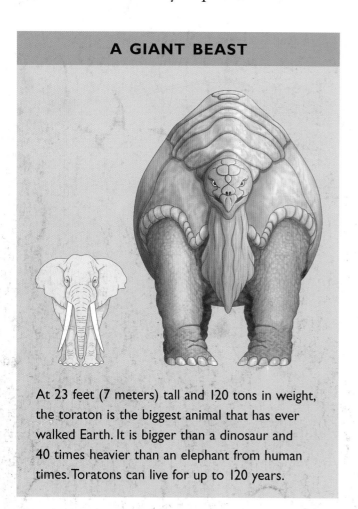

At 23 feet (7 meters) tall and 120 tons in weight, the toraton is the biggest animal that has ever walked Earth. It is bigger than a dinosaur and 40 times heavier than an elephant from human times. Toratons can live for up to 120 years.

▷ A family of toratons treads heavily across a dry part of the Bengal Swamp. Their flat, wide feet support their huge weight and stop them from sinking into the mud.

EVOLUTION IN ACTION

Toratons **evolved** from the tortoises of human times and are similar to them in many ways. Like tortoises, toratons move slowly. They also feed by tearing plants with their beak-like mouths. However, the toraton has no predators, so it no longer needs a protective shell. Just a few parts of the shell remain to help support its massive body.

◁ The giant tortoise was the biggest tortoise in human times. It was just over 3 feet (1 meter) long, but it was much smaller than a toraton.

Swampus

The swampus has **adapted** perfectly to its environment, which is part land and part water. Like its **ancestor**, the eight-armed octopus, it can breathe underwater. But the swampus can also survive for up to four days on land by using a supply of **oxygen** stored in its blood.

The swampus has four long arms for grabbing food. Its other four arms have **evolved** into thick, strong pads which help it to creep along the marshy ground.

Swampuses come to land to raise their young. Here they are safe from the dangerous lurkfish. Female swampuses lay their eggs in pools of water that form in the middle of lily plants. The females live in groups, and when a mother has to return to the water to breathe, the others take turns to guard her offspring.

▽ A mother swampus lays her eggs in the same lily pool every year. When her babies hatch, she brings them food until they are big enough to fend for themselves.

SWAMPUS CAMOUFLAGE

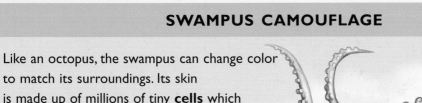

Like an octopus, the swampus can change color
to match its surroundings. Its skin
is made up of millions of tiny **cells** which
contain different colors. By opening
and closing these cells, it can create
brightly-colored patterns.

In this picture, a mother swampus
flashes up a display of bright colors to
warn larger animals, such as toratons,
to keep away from her nest. She also
uses color to disguise herself, so
she can creep up on smaller
animals while hunting.

The Antarctic Forest

The **continent** of Antarctica has moved north and now lies near the **equator**. As it moved away from the South **Pole**, its **climate** began to change. Antarctica was once a freezing land, populated by sea birds and penguins. Now, it is a warm, tropical island, covered by a rich rainforest, like the Amazon rainforest of human times.

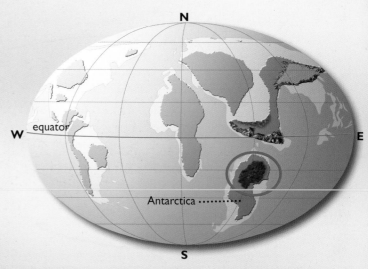

△ The Antarctic Forest covers a vast area in the northern part of Antarctica.

Birds of the Antarctic

Millions of sea birds lived on the Antarctic continent during human times. As Antarctica moved from a cold, dry climate to a warm, wet climate, only a few kinds of birds survived the changing conditions. The survivors were the most **adaptable** birds, the long-distance fliers used to moving between cold and warm areas. As the climate became warmer, their numbers grew. These sea birds eventually **evolved** into a group of forest birds called flutterbirds.

Roachcutter

One of the **descendants** of the original Antarctic sea birds is the roachcutter, a small bird with a purple body and blue and green wings. The roachcutter is an excellent flier. Its short, wide wings are perfect for making tight turns in the thick forest. Good eyesight is also essential in a forest and the roachcutter's eyes stand out from its head, giving it all-round vision.

▷ This roachcutter is a type of flutterbird. Its ability to fly quickly is an excellent defense against **predators** that live in the forest.

△ The spitfire bird is another type of flutterbird. It is slightly bigger than the roachcutter and has bright red and orange flashes on its wings. Behind it, a giant **insect** zooms in for a sudden attack.

Spitfire bird

Like rainforests in human times, the Antarctic Forest is packed with thousands of different types of life. With so many animals competing with each other for space and food, it is important to have good defenses against predators. The spitfire bird has an excellent method of self-defense. It has its own **chemical** weapon. The spitfire bird collects chemicals from flowers and stores them in a special compartment in its throat. When it finds itself under attack, it mixes up chemicals from its nose and throat to produce a deadly acid, which it sprays at its attacker. Blinded by the acid, the attacker falls to the ground, and the spitfire bird can make its escape.

EVOLUTION IN ACTION

Throughout the story of life on Earth, animals have developed amazing forms of self-defense. Spitfire birds shoot out acid to ward off their enemies. In human times, the bombardier beetle sprayed a boiling-hot liquid at attackers. As the liquid was released, it made a loud popping sound.

△ The bombardier beetle rarely missed its target. It could point its deadly spray in any direction.

△ Imagine a wasp as big as a crow! The falconfly is a giant wasp with long wings and grasping claws for hunting and killing flutterbirds. It also has powerful jaws for tearing and chewing meat from its **prey**.

Insects of the forest

The deadliest **predator** in the Antarctic Forest is a giant wasp, called a falconfly. It is one of the largest **insects** ever to live on Earth and it is also one of the most ferocious. The falconfly hunts and kills flutterbirds. To catch a strong, fast bird without damaging its own body, the falconfly must kill quickly. As soon as it sees a flutterbird, it dives in for the attack. Its hooked legs grasp the bird's body, while a second pair of legs come together to form a sharp harpoon. The falconfly spears the flutterbird, killing it immediately, and the two tumble to the ground. The giant wasp eats part of the meat itself. It takes the rest to feed its larvae, or grubs, which are hidden in burrows throughout the forest.

Spitfire beetle

Insects are the most successful predators of the Antarctic Forest. Even small insects, such as the spitfire beetle, can trap and kill a bird. To catch their prey, four spitfire beetles meet head-to-head on the trunk of a tree, forming the shape of a cross. By spreading their orange and yellow wings, they mimic, or copy, the appearance of a flower. This makes them irresistible to birds, which fly in to feed on the flower and are trapped and killed by the beetles. Copying the appearance of another object or animal is called **mimicry**.

EVOLUTION IN ACTION

Animals use mimicry for different reasons. Some creatures disguise themselves as leaves to hide from predators. Others mimic objects to trap food. The orchid mantis of human times was the same color as an orchid flower. Its body looked like the flower's petals. When the mantis sat on the orchid, it was difficult to tell the two apart. Insects came to drink but ended up as dinner!

△ Which was the orchid and which was the mantis? Look for the head at the bottom of the picture!

▷ If a bird lands on this flower, it will get a nasty surprise. The flower is not a flower at all, but four spitfire beetles, working together to trap their victim.

The Great Plateau

Nestling high up among the peaks of the highest mountain range on Earth, there is a flat region of snow and rock called the Great Plateau. The peaks were formed when two of Earth's **plates** crashed into one another, causing the land to crush together and rise up. These new mountains are very unstable. Their slopes are covered with gravel, which crumbles and slides down to the sea at the slightest wind. This makes it difficult for plants to put down roots on the mountainside.

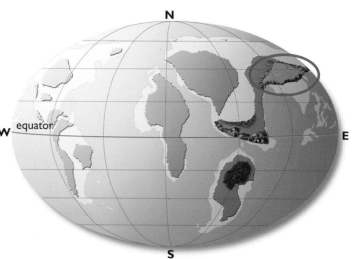

△ The vast, mountainous region of the Great Plateau rises up out of the sea like a massive block of stone.

▽ The **valleys** between the jagged peaks have filled up with rock and gravel to form a high **plateau**. At 33,000 feet (10,000 meters), the mountains of the Great Plateau are higher than any mountains from human times.

Great blue windrunner

It is difficult for animals to survive at this great height. The air is thin and there is less **oxygen** to breathe. The sun is dazzlingly bright and can easily damage the eyes of the animals that live here.

One creature that has **adapted** to these conditions is the great blue windrunner. It is a large bird with metallic-blue feathers that help to reflect the damaging sunlight. The bird also needs protection for its eyes. It could easily go blind in the piercing sun. It has **evolved** a thin, transparent layer of darker skin which it can slide across its eyes like a pair of sunglasses.

▽ Great blue windrunners fly huge distances to find food in these snow-covered peaks. Their long, narrow wings, like those of a jet plane, are ideal for soaring and gliding at high speeds.

A BIRD WITH FOUR WINGS

Long, narrow wings are perfect for long-distance flying, but when the great blue windrunner spots food, it must slow down and swoop in for the kill. To fly slowly, it needs broad wings, like those of a stunt plane. As the bird brakes, it does the splits, stretching out its feathered legs. These legs act as extra 'wings', forming a broad surface. They are ideal for turning and swooping in mid air.

▽ A great blue windrunner brings back a giant spider to feed to her young. The birds nest high in the mountain peaks of the Great Plateau.

61

Silver spider

Across the **valleys** and **gorges** of the Great Plateau, silky nets billow in the wind. These are the giant webs of silver spiders, which live among the rocks in a **colony**, or group. Each silver spider has a job to do in this highly-organized society. The youngest spiders are web builders. They spin huge webs to catch clouds of grass seeds that float through the valley. Other spiders scurry about the web, gathering up the seeds or attending to the queen. Silver spiders come in all shapes and sizes. The youngest are only a few millimeters across, but the queen can grow to the size of a football.

△ The body of a silver spider is metallic in color to reflect the sun's harmful rays. Dark stripes give it the appearance of a grass seed flying through the valley. This **camouflage** helps to confuse **predators**.

▽ Silver spiders scuttle about their web. These giant webs are the largest ever built, stretching to widths of 99 feet (30 meters). To spin them, the spiders need up to 14 miles (24 kilometers) of silk.

COLLECTING SEEDS
Forager spiders collect grass seeds. They store the seeds in special sacs before carrying them back to the mountain.

SEED RIDING
A tiny spider hitches a ride on a grass seed. Carried by the wind, it will try to land on the other side of the valley.

Finding food

Like all spiders, silver spiders are meat-eaters. So, why do they gather so many grass seeds from their web? The answer is that the spiders do not eat the seeds themselves. Instead, they harvest the seeds as food for another animal. Back in the dark caves and crevices of the mountains, small furry **mammals** snuffle about the piles of seeds, stuffing them into their fat cheeks. These cute animals are poggles. They are being fattened up to provide food for the spider queen!

PARACHUTES
The grass seed acts as a parachute for the tiny silver spider. Many young spiders do not survive their dangerous journey.

ANCHOR THREAD
As the spider flies across the valley, it releases a thick thread of silk. This anchor thread acts as a tightrope for other spiders, which soon hurry across, spinning more strands as they go.

FLYING SEEDS
Clouds of grass seeds waft up through the valleys from the foothills of the Great Plateau to be caught in the huge webs.

△ A poggle feasts on a pile of seeds left by the spiders. Although poggles are sacrificed as food for the queen, they have a close partnership with the spiders, which provide them with a constant supply of seeds.

200 MILLION YEARS

Two hundred million years in the future, all of Earth's **continents** have finally crashed together, forming a single giant continent known as Pangaea II. If there is only one continent, there can only be one ocean. Pangaea II is surrounded by a mighty body of water called the Global Ocean. This is a world of thick forests, scorched deserts and deep waters, inhabited by all sorts of strange creatures. It is a world of unimaginable extremes.

▽ This map shows what our world might look like in 200 million years.

W   equator

Northern Forest

Rain falls constantly on the northwest coast of Pangaea II. In this rich, damp region, a strong, vibrant forest has sprung up, which is bursting with life.

Earth in human times

In human times, the seven continents of Earth were spread about the globe. Surrounding the continents, there were four great oceans and many smaller seas. Many continents were completely cut off by water. Two hundred million years in the future, Earth's surface is divided between one huge continent and a single, vast ocean.

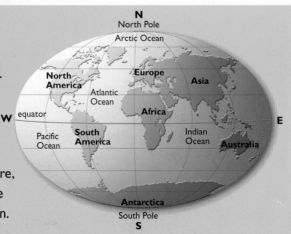

N
North Pole
Arctic Ocean

North America

Europe

Asia

Atlantic Ocean

W   equator   Africa   E

Pacific Ocean

South America

Indian Ocean

Australia

Antarctica
South Pole
S

MAP KEY

land areas

forest

mountains

desert

ocean

Central Desert

Pangaea II is so huge that no rain ever reaches its center. As a result, most of the continent is dominated by the Central Desert, the largest desert that has ever existed.

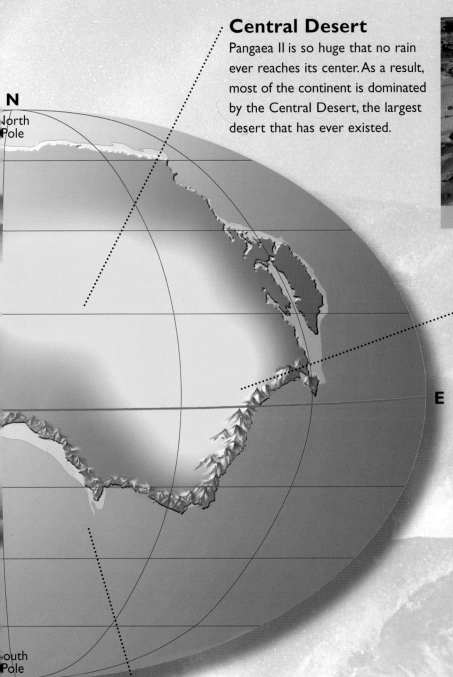

N
North Pole

E

South Pole

S

Rainshadow Desert

Around the south coast of Pangaea II, a towering mountain range acts as a barrier against the constant storms that roll in from the sea. The Rainshadow Desert lies in the shade of these stormy peaks.

Global Ocean

The Global Ocean is an immense, unbroken expanse of water. The ocean **currents** cover huge distances, making it easy for sea animals to move around.

The Central Desert

Imagine a desert that covers an area five times bigger than the entire USA was in human times. This is the huge, hostile Central Desert, the largest desert ever! There are no clouds here and it never rains. The sun beats down all day long and temperatures often reach a scorching 122°F (50°C). Nights are bone-chillingly cold, dropping to –22°F (–30°C). Although the desert's surface is totally dry, deep underground, there is a network of water-filled caves. It is thanks to this reservoir of water that animals can survive here.

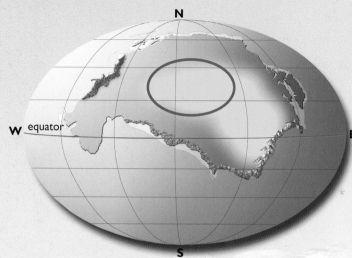

△ The Central Desert stretches across a wide belt of land in the middle of Pangaea II. It is more than twice as big as the Sahara Desert in Africa in human times.

▷ Terabytes live in tall, sandy mounds dotted around the desert. No terabytes have legs, except for the transporters. Other terabytes, such as warriors, rely on the transporters to carry them from place to place.

EVOLUTION IN ACTION

Terabytes are **insects**. They are the most successful creatures in the Central Desert. Throughout Earth's history, insects have been the best survivors. Like other insects, terabytes are perfectly **adapted** for survival in extreme **climates**. Their small size allows them to live in the tiniest nooks and crannies. They also have a tough armor on the outside of their soft bodies which seals in moisture and prevents them from drying out. This makes it possible for terabytes to live in the driest of places.

▷ In human times, termites were insects that lived together in large groups. Here they are working together to fix a hole in their nest.

Terabyte

Armies of terabytes march across the hot desert floor. Their **ancestors** were termites, which lived all over the world in human times. Terabytes live in large groups, called **colonies**. Each member of the colony spends its life looking after the queen. The survival of the queen is essential because she is the only terabyte that breeds. She must produce eggs constantly for the colony to succeed.

Desert cities

Terabyte mounds rise up out of the gravelly earth, towering above the tiny **insects**. Inside, they are like bustling cities. Each mound is a sophisticated feat of construction and engineering. The cool air circulating inside means they even have air-conditioning! But the jagged, dusty towers are only part of the terabytes' home. Underground, in a network of tunnels and chambers, the terabytes breed, dig for water and harvest food.

A job to do

The terabyte **colony** is organized into groups, called castes. There are seven castes in all and each one has a job to do. Builders construct the walls of the mound by gathering grains of sand and pasting them together. Warriors guard the mound from enemies, shooting deadly acid from nozzles in their heads when under threat. Transporters carry builders and warriors from place to place. Inside the nest, rock-borers dig tunnels, while water carriers deliver water for everyone. Nurses collect food for the queen, who is the leader of the entire colony.

▷ Here you can see the tunnels and chambers that make up the terabytes' home. The terabytes grow food in the top part of the mound, which is a bit like a farm. Their living quarters are deep in the rock.

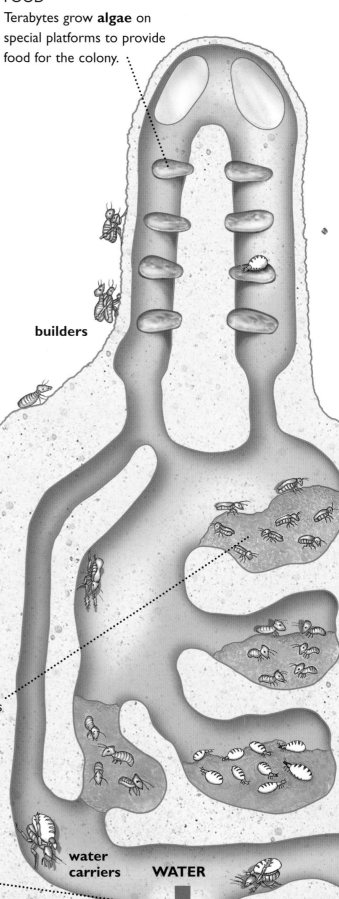

FOOD
Terabytes grow **algae** on special platforms to provide food for the colony.

builders

carriers

NEST
Nests, where the terabytes care for their young, are dotted around the inside of the mound.

WATER WELL
Long tunnels lead to water, deep underground. Water carriers make the difficult journey to collect the water. They bring it back inside their bloated bellies.

water carriers   **WATER**

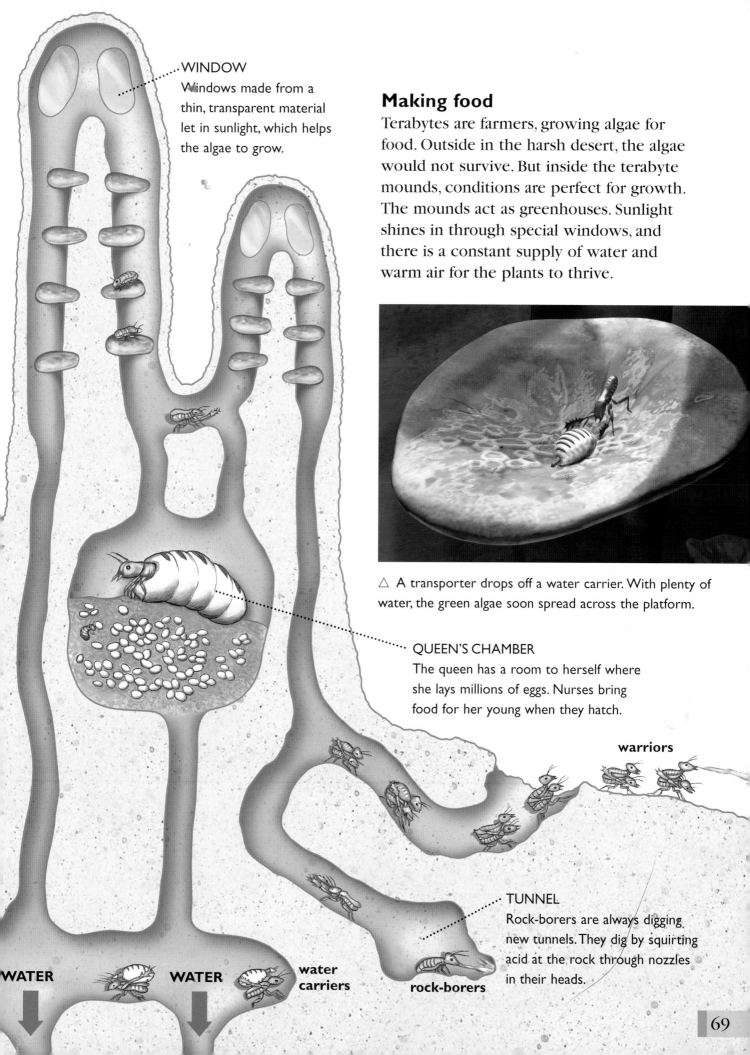

WINDOW
Windows made from a thin, transparent material let in sunlight, which helps the algae to grow.

Making food

Terabytes are farmers, growing algae for food. Outside in the harsh desert, the algae would not survive. But inside the terabyte mounds, conditions are perfect for growth. The mounds act as greenhouses. Sunlight shines in through special windows, and there is a constant supply of water and warm air for the plants to thrive.

△ A transporter drops off a water carrier. With plenty of water, the green algae soon spread across the platform.

QUEEN'S CHAMBER
The queen has a room to herself where she lays millions of eggs. Nurses bring food for her young when they hatch.

warriors

TUNNEL
Rock-borers are always digging new tunnels. They dig by squirting acid at the rock through nozzles in their heads.

WATER   **WATER**   **water carriers**

rock-borers

Lurking underground

Terabytes are not the only animals that live in the Central Desert. Deep underground, in a maze of water-filled caves, there are other, stranger, creatures. The garden worm, the gloom worm and the slickribbon look different, but they all come from the same **ancestor**, a type of worm known as a bristleworm. In human times, bristleworms lived in the oceans. Over millions of years, they have **evolved** into the three types of worm that now live in the caves below the desert.

Garden worm

Every day, one of these cave-dwelling worms, the garden worm, comes up to the desert's surface. Its body is divided into segments, or parts. It arches its body and begins to unfurl green, fern-like branches from each segment. These branches contain **algae**, which are plants. Like all plants, the algae need the sun's energy to make food for themselves. The garden worm relies on this food for its own survival, so it must spend part of each day sunbathing, and helping the algae to grow!

▽ A garden worm basks in the hot desert sun. It is difficult to tell if this creature is a plant, or an animal, or both.

MAKING FOOD

sunlight

carbon
dioxide

water

Plants, including the algae inside the garden worm, need sunlight, water and a gas called carbon dioxide to make food. A plant's leaves take in carbon dioxide while water is soaked up through the roots. Green **cells** in the leaves absorb sunlight and use the sun's energy to turn carbon dioxide and water into food. This process is called **photosynthesis**.

Slickribbon

Unlike the garden worm, the slickribbon never ventures out into the sunlight. This giant **predator** lives permanently in the dark underwater caves. It is about 3 feet (1 meter) long and, like the garden worm, its body is divided into segments. Attached to each segment, there is a pair of hairy paddles. By beating these paddles in a continuous, wave-like motion, the slickribbon shoots through the water at high speeds.

The slickribbon spends most of its time lurking in the murky water, hunting for food. Its favorite snack is the gloomworm, a smaller worm that crawls along the cave walls. From time to time, the slickribbon grabs a bigger, tastier prize, a garden worm caught sleeping in the caves at night.

▽ The giant slickribbon is a swift predator. It moves so quickly that a gloomworm has no chance to escape before it is snapped up in a pair of powerful jaws.

The Global Ocean

The Global Ocean is a massive, warm sea covering nearly three-quarters of the planet. If you were dropped in the middle, you would have to swim 9,600 miles (16,000 kilometers) to the shore. You would be swimming for more than a year! Strong winds whip up the ocean **currents**, carrying sea animals long distances. They travel so far that similar types of sea creatures are found all over the Global Ocean.

△ The Global Ocean is a great body of water that completely surrounds the giant continent of Pangaea II.

Silverswimmer

After the time of the humans, many sea creatures died out. One group that survived was the arthropods, which included animals such as crabs, lobsters and shrimps. The secret of their success was that their larvae, or grubs, could feed on all kinds of food and live in many different conditions. As the planet changed, they **adapted** to suit their new surroundings. Over millions of years, they **evolved** into silverswimmers.

In the Global Ocean, there are at least 9,000 **species** of silverswimmer. Like arthropods from human times, they have flexible, jointed legs. They also have a tail that moves up and down to help them swim and a tough shell-like covering to protect their bodies. Silverswimmers are filter-feeders, which means they sieve tiny sea creatures, called plankton, from the water, to eat. Every summer, they lay thousands of eggs. The eggs float in the water for four days before hatching.

▽ These silverswimmers are about 6 inches
(15 centimeters) long, which is about the size
of sardines in human times. They swim together
through the sea in large groups called shoals.

Ocean flish

In human times, the oceans were filled with thousands of kinds of fish. Two hundred million years later, only a few kinds have survived and they have changed so much that they are almost unrecognizable. They are the fierce, flying ocean flish. Unlike most of their **ancestors**, flish can breathe air. They have tough, protective skin, and their fins have become powerful wings that allow them to fly fast across the surface of the sea. They do this to hunt for silverswimmers, which they snap up instantly from just beneath the waves. Ocean flish live in groups and make their nests on land.

EVOLUTION IN ACTION

In human times, there were 'flying fish' that could travel through the air for a short time to escape from underwater enemies. They used their strong tails to propel themselves out of the water, then glided through the air on their broad fins.
The ocean flish's fins have **evolved** even further. They have grown stronger and developed into real wings that keep the flish up by flapping.

△ Although flying fish from human times could only glide and not fly properly, a few kinds could cover the length of a football field in the air!

Why has the flish learned to fly?

Two hundred million years in the future, birds have died out. When they disappeared, they left the skies empty and available for other animals. The ocean flish has **evolved** to fill this gap, or **niche**, by developing the ability to fly. This has given the ocean flish huge advantages. It can now travel at high speed and cover large areas in its search for food. It can also easily make a quick escape from dangerous ocean **predators**.

Similar changes have taken place throughout Earth's history. Many types of animals have **adapted** to suit new living spaces. One hundred and fifty million years before human times, a few types of dinosaurs grew feathers, developed lighter bodies and became birds. This new family of animals dominated the skies for many millions of years.

△ This creature, called an archaeopteryx, was a dinosaur-like animal with bird's feathers. It lived about 150 million years ago. Many scientists believe that archaeopteryx was the first bird.

▽ An ocean flish plunges into the waves to catch a silverswimmer. To grab its **prey** from below the surface of the water, it has a pair of long, narrow jaws tipped with sharp fangs. The jaws shoot out from inside the flish's mouth, targeting its victim with deadly accuracy.

△ Sharkopaths, which are a type of shark, work together to trap a huge animal called a rainbow squid. After killing their **prey**, they eat as much of it as they can. They will not need to eat again for another three months.

Sharkopaths on the hunt

Sharks have ruled the oceans for millions of years, and life is no different in the Global Ocean. In this future world, sharks have become even more efficient and deadly **predators**, known as sharkopaths. Their streamlined body shape is similar to a shark's body from human times. But they also have an extra feature – glowing bands of light on the sides of their bodies.

In human times, sharks hunted alone. However, food is spread out and difficult to find in this huge ocean, so the sharkopaths hunt in packs. They use the glowing patches to signal to each other that food is nearby. Then they begin to close in on their victim. This method allows them to kill creatures much larger than themselves.

EVOLUTION IN ACTION

In human times, a few kinds of deep-sea fish had bioluminescent, or glowing, patches on their bodies. They included the deep-sea angler fish and the spined pygmy shark. The angler fish used the bright light on its head to lure prey in the dark, while the spined pygmy shark had lights on its stomach which acted as **camouflage**. Sharkopaths use their glowing spots as a sophisticated signalling tool.

△ The light patches on the tiny spined pygmy shark disguised the outline of its body. When seen from below, the shark blended in with the water around it.

Rainbow squid

The rainbow squid is the giant of the Global Ocean. Its body is 66 feet (20 meters) long, and its arms extend for another 66 feet (20 meters). That's as long as eight elephants and twice as big as any giant squid from human times. Like other giant squids, the rainbow squid has eyes the size of footballs to help it to see in the depths of the dark ocean. At the center of its eight long, thick arms lies its powerful, flesh-tearing beak. It is a fierce **carnivore**, which uses its amazing **camouflage** to sneak up on prey. The rainbow squid can merge with the dark blue of the sea or even create a rippling pattern on its skin to disguise itself as a shoal of silverswimmers. When it is close to its food, it shoots out two powerful tentacles, grabbing its victim and dragging it into its mouth.

△ A rainbow squid descends into the deep ocean, turning its skin a pale color to blend in with the sunlit water. Its arms and tentacles are lined with hundreds of suckers which help it to grip its prey tightly.

EVOLUTION IN ACTION

The rainbow squid can change color at will to hide itself or to produce amazing displays. In human times, squids could also change color. Thousands of tiny **cells** in their skin contained different colors called pigments. The squid opened or closed the cells to reveal the pigments. This created spectacular patterns on their bodies. The rainbow squid adds complex fluorescent effects to its displays.

◁ A squid from human times used its color displays to communicate.

△ Once a year, on the night of a full moon, rainbow squids gather together to mate. They light up the ocean with amazing displays. In this picture, a male rainbow squid has attracted a female to his side with his brightly-colored, flashing body.

The Rainshadow Desert

The Rainshadow Desert is an endless, dusty plain, dotted with clumps of yellow grass and scrubby bushes. Survival here is extremely tough, because there is little water. The Rainshadow Desert lies behind a huge coastal mountain range. Massive windstorms often carry ocean plants and animals over the mountains and into the desert, providing food for desert creatures.

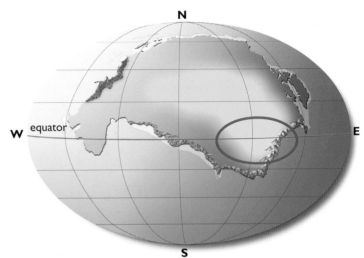

△ The Rainshadow Desert lies in the east of Pangaea II, close to the stormy coast of the Global Ocean. The desert is hot during the day and cold at night.

HOW DOES A RAINSHADOW DESERT GET ITS NAME?

A rainshadow desert gets its name because it lies in the shadow of a mountain range. The mountains form a barrier, with the desert on one side and the sea on the other. Rain clouds blow in from the ocean and rise up the mountain peaks, but the rain almost always falls before it can reach the desert on the other side. As a result, the desert is permanently dry. There were several rainshadow deserts on Earth in human times, including the Mojave Desert in North America.

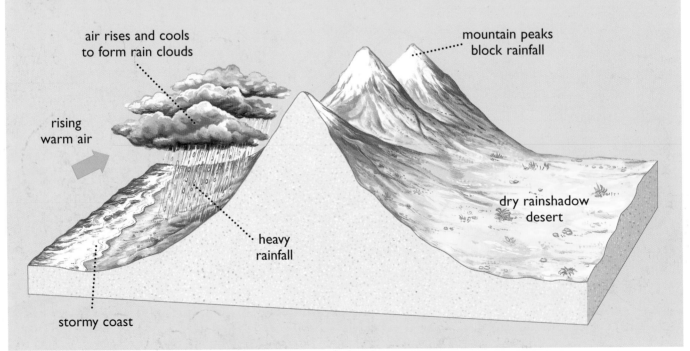

air rises and cools to form rain clouds

mountain peaks block rainfall

rising warm air

heavy rainfall

dry rainshadow desert

stormy coast

Desert hopper

Across the desert's surface, creatures the size of rabbits hop from bush to bush, munching on the tough leaves. But these are not rabbits, they are a type of snail called the desert hopper. Like snails from human times, the desert hopper has a hard shell for protection and a strong, muscular 'foot' to help it move. But instead of crawling, the desert hopper leaps along at roughly the same pace as a human walking. Unlike other land snails, it does not leave behind a trail of slime. In this dry environment, it needs to keep as much moisture as possible inside its body, to prevent it from drying out in the desert heat.

▽ Desert hoppers feed on plants. They have a powerful tongue, called a radula, which is covered in sharp teeth. This allows them to pierce the tough surfaces of desert plants. These hoppers can devour a bush in a few hours.

EVOLUTION IN ACTION

The desert hopper has **evolved** the ability to hop to help it cope with its environment. In the desert, food is scarce and animals need to travel long distances to find it. By hopping, the desert hopper can move faster and cover more ground. Hopping also lessens the amount of contact between the snail's foot and the hot desert surface.

△ Although it was unusual, in human times, there were snails that could hop, although they only lived underwater. This marine cone snail is one example.

Meet the bumblebeetle

A loud buzzing noise fills the still air of the Rainshadow Desert. It is a large flying **insect** called a bumblebeetle. This insect has only one aim in life: to find the dead ocean flish that are carried into the desert by winds from the sea. The bumblebeetle has ultra-sensitive antennae, or feelers, to pick up the slightest whiff of a flish's body from many miles away. This is vital because the flish are scattered across the desert. Powered by a store of fat which takes up almost half of its body, a bumblebeetle can travel up to 480 miles (800 kilometers) in one day, which is the equivalent of an 8-hour car journey.

▷ This bumblebeetle has found a dead ocean flish. Instead of eating it, the bumblebeetle gives birth to a litter of tiny grubs here. The grubs feed on the flish and grow fatter. Eventually, they turn into adult bumblebeetles that fly off in search of other flish to make their own babies.

The Northern Forest

Along the coast of Pangaea II, there is a hot, damp, swampy rainforest. Massive trees, taller than any from human times, stand side by side in the rich, **fertile** soil. The trees are so close together that, in the depths of the forest, sunlight barely filters through the leaves. It rains almost constantly here. Dark clouds, full of moisture, roll in from the ocean, breaking over the forest. The warm, wet conditions are perfect for all kinds of animals to thrive.

Forest flish

High in the leafy tree-tops of the Northern Forest, brightly-colored creatures flit from branch to branch. They are so tiny that they could sit in the palm of your hand. These creatures are forest flish, a type of fish that has **adapted** to life on land. Forest flish are related to the ocean flish we met on page 74. But unlike ocean flish, which return to the sea to hunt, forest flish spend their entire lives among the trees, snapping up **insects** from the branches in their long, thin beaks or even plucking them from mid air.

Forest flish communicate by chirruping. They produce sound in a similar way to grasshoppers in human times. Grasshoppers rubbed their legs and wings together to produce a chirruping noise. Forest flish rub together special teeth at the back of their throats. This sets off a vibration which leads to the loud, shrill trilling sound they make.

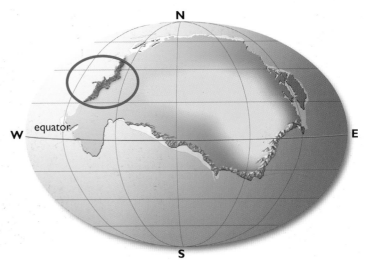

△ The Northern Forest stretches for thousands of miles along the northwest coast of Pangaea II.

EVOLUTION IN ACTION

In many ways, forest flish resemble hummingbirds, which were small forest birds that lived during human times. Like hummingbirds, forest flish flap their wings so quickly that they can hover, or stay still, in mid air. They are also extremely fast flyers, darting through the forest at high speed and dodging any **predators** that come near.

△ In human times, hummingbirds ate insects and nectar from flowers. They could flap their wings up to 70 times per second and even fly backwards!

△ Forest flish roost in the tree-tops, hanging upside
down under the branches. In this position, under the
leafy canopy, they are sheltered from the constant rain.

From sea to land

Far below the lofty home of the forest flish, a giant strides across the forest floor. This is a megasquid. It is an invertebrate, which means it has no backbone or skeleton. It belongs to a class of animals called cephalopods. In human times, cephalopods, such as squids and octopuses, lived in the ocean. Now, 200 million years in the future, they have left the ocean and moved to the land. This is not so surprising. The **ancestors** of all land-living animals originally lived in the sea. Eventually, they **evolved** to breathe air and crawled on to land. In this future world, cephalopods have done the same.

◁ A megasquid crashes through the forest, crushing everything in its path. It moves slowly, but it is so big and strong that other creatures keep well away from it.

Megasquid

The megasquid is taller than an elephant, and much heavier. It weighs a colossal 8 tons. Much of this weight comes from the heavy muscles in its eight thick legs, which need to be strong enough to support such a large body. Moving on eight legs is no easy task and the megasquid has a strange walking style. It shuffles fowards a few legs at a time, reaching speeds no faster than a human walking pace.

The megasquid is the king of the forest. Since it has no enemies, it can live for up to 50 years. As it marches through the forest, it makes a loud bellowing call to let other creatures know that this is its territory. The megasquid is not a fussy eater. It feasts on anything in its path, including leaves, shoots and other animals, which it grabs from the trees with its long, grasping tentacles.

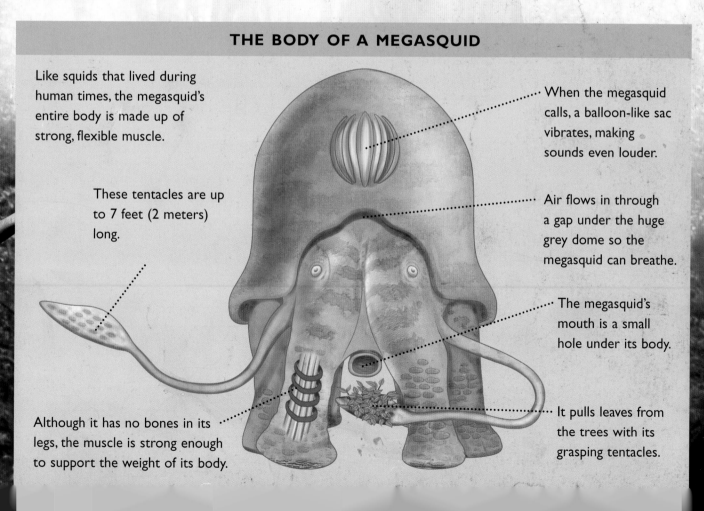

THE BODY OF A MEGASQUID

Like squids that lived during human times, the megasquid's entire body is made up of strong, flexible muscle.

These tentacles are up to 7 feet (2 meters) long.

Although it has no bones in its legs, the muscle is strong enough to support the weight of its body.

When the megasquid calls, a balloon-like sac vibrates, making sounds even louder.

Air flows in through a gap under the huge grey dome so the megasquid can breathe.

The megasquid's mouth is a small hole under its body.

It pulls leaves from the trees with its grasping tentacles.

Squibbon

Another cephalopod that has made its home in the Northern Forest is the squibbon. It is a distant relative of the megasquid, but the two are very different. Like the megasquid, the squibbon has no skeleton inside its body. But it is much smaller than its giant cousin and instead of living on the ground, it uses its muscular arms to swing through the trees.

Squibbons spend their entire lives in the trees. Their arms and tentacles are so flexible that they can grip branches and grab food with ease. They can also weave twigs and leaves into shelters, which they build in the tree-tops. They return to these shelters at night to sleep and tend to their young.

Living in such a thick forest requires a certain degree of intelligence and squibbons have **evolved** large brains to cope with their crowded **habitat**. They navigate through the trees at high speed, looking out for danger at every turn. They are sociable creatures and live in large, organized communities, sharing food and taking care of one another's babies.

▷ The squibbon's eyes are on the end of long, flexible stalks. As it somersaults through the forest, its bendy eyes stay pointing forwards, even though its body is twisting and turning.

EVOLUTION IN ACTION

Squibbons and megasquids are **descendants** of squids, which lived in the oceans during human times. Squids were well known for their bright colors, which they used to attract mates or warn off other squids. But bright colors are not much use to squibbons and megasquids because there are so many trees blocking their view. So, instead of color, they use sound to communicate.

△ Squids had eight arms and two longer tentacles with suckers to grab food. Like squibbons, they were highly intelligent and had excellent eyesight.

What does the future hold?

Now that you have met the creatures of *The Wild World of the Future*, what do you think the next 100 million years have in store for them? Will the squibbons' intelligence help them to dominate Earth, just as humans did? Or will other creatures respond and **adapt** more quickly to their changing world?

Perhaps some of the animals you have met will die out, to be replaced by other, even stranger creatures. Can you piece together clues from nature and Earth's past to build up a picture of the distant future? After all, the future could be as wild as your imagination... or even wilder!

Creature profiles

my = millions of years from now

gannetwhale (5 my)
Gannetwhales are huge birds that live in the icy oceans of Northern Europe. They spend most of their lives in the water.

snowstalker (5 my)
The snowstalker is a **mammal** that prowls across the snow-covered lands of Northern Europe. It has long, sharp teeth and white fur.

shagrat (5 my)
Shagrats are **mammals** with woolly coats to keep them warm in the icy conditions of Northern Europe. They have big, bear-like paws.

cryptile lizard (5 my)
The cryptile is a lizard that lives in the Mediterranean Basin. It has a large, sticky frill around its neck which it uses for catching food.

scrofa (5 my)
Large herds of scrofas forage for food in the rocks around the Mediterranean Basin. They are **descendants** of a type of pig called a wild boar.

gryken (5 my)
The gryken is a solitary, meat-eating **mammal** with long, sharp teeth. It hunts among the rocks around the Mediterranean Basin.

babookari (5 my)
Babookaris are highly-intelligent monkeys with red faces and long, straight tails. They live in the Amazon Grasslands.

rattleback (5 my)
Rattlebacks are **rodents** with tough, rattling scales. Their scales protect them from the fires that ravage the Amazon Grasslands.

carakiller (5 my)
Carakillers are birds. They are the fastest runners on the Amazon Grassland. They use their sharp claws and long beaks for hunting.

deathgleaner (5 my)
Deathgleaners are giant meat-eating bats. They soar above the North American Desert, searching for **prey** on the ground.

reef glider (100 my)
Multi-colored reef gliders feed on the **reefs** of the Shallow Seas. Their **ancestors** were tiny sea slugs, but reef gliders are the size of seals.

ocean phantom (100 my)
The ocean phantom floats across the Shallow Seas. It is not one jellyfish, but a massive group of jellyfish working together to survive.

spindletrooper (100 my)
Spindletroopers are **descendants** of sea spiders. They live in the tentacles of the ocean phantom in the Shallow Seas.

lurkfish (100 my)
The lurkfish lies in wait for food in the muddy waters of the Bengal Swamp. It stuns its **prey** with a sharp electric shock.

toraton (100 my)
The toraton is the largest animal ever to have walked the planet. It lives in the Bengal Swamp and is a far cry from its tiny tortoise **ancestors**!

swampus (100 my)
The swampus is a large octopus that has developed a way of surviving for several days on land. It lives in the Bengal Swamp.

roachcutter (100 my)
The roachcutter is a small, colorful bird which uses its brilliant eyesight and short wings to zoom through the Antarctic Forest.

spitfire bird (100 my)
The spitfire bird lives in the Antarctic Forest and is a close relative of the roachcutter. When under threat, it spits acid at its attacker.

falconfly (100 my)

The falconfly is a giant wasp that uses its powerful jaws and strong legs to catch and eat the birds of the Antarctic Forest.

spitfire beetle (100 my)

Spitfire beetles are brightly-colored **insects**. They gather in groups of four to mimic a flower and trap birds of the Antarctic Forest.

great blue windrunner (100 my)

The great blue windrunner is a bird with not one but two pairs of wings! It glides high above the Great Plateau and can even take a nap as it flies.

silver spider (100 my)

Silver spiders spin huge webs on the Great Plateau. They have shiny silver bodies to reflect the harsh light from the sun.

poggle (100 my)

Poggles are the last **mammals** left on the planet. They have big eyes and soft fur and live in the dark caves of the Great Plateau.

terabyte (200 my)

Terabytes are small **insects**. They are related to termites from human times. Terabytes live in **colonies** in huge mounds in the Central Desert.

garden worm (200 my)

The garden worm lives in the caves of the Central Desert. It makes its own food on long green branches which curl out from its back.

gloomworm (200 my)

Gloomworms live in the dark caverns below the Central Desert, eating the tiny bacteria that grow on the damp cave walls.

slickribbon (200 my)

The slickribbon is a long worm that swims through the water-filled caverns below the Central Desert. It eats gloomworms.

silverswimmer (200 my)

Silverswimmers are sea creatures with hard shells and many long, bristly legs. They make their home all over the Global Ocean.

ocean flish (200 my)

Flish rule the skies above the Global Ocean. Their **ancestors** were fish whose fins **evolved** into wings to help them take to the skies.

sharkopath (200 my)

Sharkopaths are related to sharks from human times and look similar. They are the main **predators** of the Global Ocean.

rainbow squid (200 my)

The rainbow squid is a giant sea animal that lives in the Global Ocean. It gets its name from its amazing displays of color.

desert hopper (200 my)

The desert hopper is a large snail that hops around on one muscular foot. It eats the tough, chewy plants of the Rainshadow Desert.

bumblebeetle (200 my)

The bumblebeetle is a large **insect** that buzzes around the skies of the Rainshadow Desert. Bumblebeetles live for less than one day.

forest flish (200 my)

Forest flish are brightly-colored creatures that live in the Northern Forest. They are **descendants** of fish but fly like birds.

megasquid (200 my)

The megasquid is a giant, air-breathing squid that crashes through the Northern Forest. It is the size and color of an elephant.

squibbon (200 my)

Squibbons are **descendants** of squids. They are intelligent, agile creatures that spend their lives high in the trees of the Northern Forest.

Glossary

adapt To change. Living things slowly adapt, or change, to suit the landscape and weather conditions around them. This helps them to survive in their changing environment.

algae Simple plants with no roots or leaves that grow in water. Seaweeds are algae.

ancestor An animal's ancestor is a member of its family that lived long ago and from whom it is descended. For example, dinosaurs may have been the ancestors of birds.

camouflage The markings or colors on an animal that help it to blend in with its surroundings and hide from other animals.

carnivore An animal that eats meat.

cell The smallest part of an animal or plant. Most animals are made up millions of cells. The simplest living things have only one cell.

chemical A substance used by animals and plants that reacts with another substance. The spitfire beetle shoots out a deadly chemical to defend itself from attackers.

climate The usual pattern of weather from one year to the next found in a particular place in the world.

colony A large group of creatures that live and work together.

continent One of the large areas of land on Earth. The world has seven continents, which are Africa, Asia, Europe, North America, South America, Australia and Antarctica.

crust The solid outer surface of the Earth.

current A river of water that moves through the ocean from one place to another.

descendant A member of a family of living things that has developed from an **ancestor** that lived a long time ago.

equator An imaginary line around the middle of the Earth.

evolve To develop or change slowly over millions of years. As animals and plants evolve, they can turn into new **species**.

extinct No longer living on Earth. An animal becomes extinct when there are no more of its kind left on Earth.

fertile Soil that is able to grow healthy plants.

fossil The ancient remains of plants and animals preserved in rock.

gills The special **organs** that an underwater animal, such as a fish, uses for breathing.

glacier A huge, slow-moving river of ice.

gorge A deep and narrow **valley**.

habitat The natural surroundings where an animal or plant lives.

herbivore An animal that eats plants.

insect A small animal with six legs and a hard outer body. Many insects have wings.

mammal A warm-blooded animal, such as a human, dog or whale, that gives birth to live babies and feeds them milk. Most mammals are hairy. Bats are the only mammals that can fly.

mantle The thick layer of rock between the Earth's **crust** and the core.

mimicry Copying the appearance of another object or animal. Animals copy other objects to help defend themselves or to hunt **prey**.

mineral A substance formed naturally in rocks. Salt and coal are both minerals.

niche Every living thing has its niche, which is made up of where it lives, what it feeds on and what it needs to survive. When a niche becomes free, animals often **evolve** to fill it.

nutrient A substance that helps a plant or animal to grow.

omnivore An animal that eats both plants and other animals.

organ A part of an animal that has its own special function. Lungs are an organ that animals use for breathing.

organism An individual living thing, such as a plant or an animal.

oxygen One of the gases in the air, which animals and plants need to live.

photosynthesis The process that a plant uses to make food. Plants need water, energy from the sun and carbon dioxide to make food.

plate A huge piece of the Earth's **crust** that floats on the **mantle**.

plateau A generally flat area of high land.

poles The farthest points north and south on the Earth.

predator An animal that hunts and eats other animals for food.

prey An animal that is hunted by another animal for food is called its prey.

reef A long line of underwater rocks or coral, close to the surface of the sea.

reptile A cold-blooded animal with scaly skin that gives birth by laying eggs. Snakes and lizards are reptiles.

rodent One of a group of small **mammals** with large front teeth used for gnawing. Mice, rats and squirrels are all rodents.

species A group of plants or animals that can breed together and often share similar physical features.

symbiotic relationship A close relationship between two living things which benefits both.

tornado A violent storm with strong circular winds and a funnel-shaped cloud.

torpor A half-sleeping state that animals such as bats use to save energy.

tundra A flat and treeless land with permanently frozen soil.

valley The low land between mountains.

wingspan The spread of a flying animal's wings, from one wingtip to the other.

Index

Page numbers in *italic* type refer to illustrations.

A

adaptation 6, 10, 15, 17, 20-1, 24, 28, 52, 54, 72, 74, 92
albatross 15, *15*
algae 42, 44, *44*, 47, 48, 68, 69, *69*, 70-1, 92
Amazon Grasslands 23, 34-7
amphibian 12
angler fish 76
ant 16, *16*
Antarctic Forest 41, 54-7
arachnid 13
archaeopteryx 74, *74*
arthropod 13, 72

B

babookari 34-5, *34-5*, 90
barbel *49*
bat 38-9, *39*
beetle 13, 55, *55*
Bengal Swamp 40, 48-53
bioluminescence 76, 78, *78-9*
bird 12, 14, 15, 24-5, *25*, 36, 54-5, 59-61, 74, *74*, 84
bird of prey 11, *11*, 36
blue tit 15, *15*
body temperature 10, 13, 25, 26, 27
bombardier beetle 55, *55*
bristleworm 70
bumblebeetle 82, *82-3*, 90
bushfire 34, 35, 36

C

camel 10, 11, *11*
camouflage 26, 28, 33, 49, 53, *53*, 62, 76, *76*, 77, 78, 92
carakiller 36, *36-7*, 90
carnivore 42, 77, 92
caste 68

cell 19, *19*, 53, 71, 78, 92
Central Desert 65, 66-71
cephalopod 13, 87-8
chemical defense 55, *55*, 92
climate 8-9, 20, 28, 92
cold blooded 12, 13
colony 44-7, 62, 66-9, 92
communication 34, 76, 78, 84, 88
coniferous forest 10, *10*
continent 4, 6-7, *6*, 8-9, *8-9*, 40, 64-5, 92
core, Earth's 4, *4*
crab 72
crocodile 13, *13*, 19
crust, Earth's 4, 5, 92
cryptile lizard 28, *29*, *30-1*, 90
current 65, 72, 92

D

deathgleaner 38-9, *38*, *39*, 90
deciduous woodland 11, *11*
defense 55, *55*
desert 10, 11, *11*, 38-9, 66-71, 80-3
desert hopper 81, *81*, 90
dinosaur 7, 19, 74
dolphin 15

E

earthquake 4
electric fish 49
elephant 11, *11*, 16, *16*
elk 10, *10*
emu 36
equator 6, 8, *8-9*, 22, *22*, 54, 92
evolution 7, 14-19, 20, 22, 25, 27, 30, 32, 42, 47, 51, 52, 54, 70, 72, 74, 76, 81, 84, 87, 88, 92
exoskeleton 13
extinct species 16, 22, 92

F

falconfly 56, *56*, 90
filter-feeders 72
fish 12, 15, 16, 18, 42, 49, 74, *74*, 76
flutterbird 54-5
fly 28, 29
flying fish 74, *74*
forest flish 84, *85*, 90
fossil 18-19, *18*, 92
frilled lizard 30, *30*
frog 16, *16*

G

Galápagos Islands 17
gannetwhale 24-5, *24-5*, 90
garden worm 70-1, *70*, *71*, 90
gastropod 13
gazelle 16, *16*
gene 19
gill 42, 92
glacier 24, 26, 92
Global Ocean 64, 65, 72-9
gloomworm 70, 71, 90
grasshopper 84
grassland 11, *11*, 34-7
great blue windrunner 59-61, *59*, *60-1*, 90
Great Plateau 41, 58-63
gryke 32-3
gryken 33, *33*, 90

H

habitat 10-11, *10-11*, 17, 20, 88, 92
herbivore 50, 93
heron 10, *10*
Himalayas 5, *5*
human 16, 18, 19, *19*
hummingbird 84, *84*

I

Ice Age 22-39
iceberg 24
Iceland 5, *5*
iguana 10, *10*
insect 13, 16, 19, 28, 55-6,
 55, 56, 57, 66-9, 82, 93
invertebrate 12, 13, 18, 87

K

karst 32
kiwi 14, *14*

L

lily 52, *52*
limestone 32
lizard 11, 28-31
lobster 72
lurkfish 49, *49,* 52, 90

M

mammal 12, 19, 93
mantle 4, *4,* 93
mating display 28, *31, 78-9*
Mediterranean Basin 23, 28-33
megasquid *86,* 87, *87,* 90
mimicry 56, *56, 57,* 93
mite 13
Mojave Desert 80
mollusc 13
monkey 34
monsoon 9, *9*
mountain 5, *5,* 11, *11,* 58-63, 80
musk ox 10, *10*

N

niche 14, 74, 93
North American Desert 22, 38-9
Northern Forest 64, 84-9
North European Ice 23, 24-7

O

ocean flish 74-5, *75,* 82, 90
ocean phantom 44-7, *44-5, 46-7,* 90
octopus 13, 52, 87
omnivore 32, 35, 93
orchid mantis 56, *56*

ostrich 36
oxygen 42, 59, 93

P

pampa 11
Pangaea II 7, *7,* 64-5
penguin 15, 25, *25,* 54
photosynthesis 71, *71,* 93
pig 32, *32*
plankton 72
plate, Earth's 4-6, *4, 5,* 40, 58, 93
poggle 63, *63,* 90
Poles 6, 8, 10, 22, *23,* 40
porcupine 35
Portuguese man-of-war 45, *45*
prairie 11
predator 14, 20, 24, 27, 33,
 49, 51, 56, 93
pygmy shark 76, *76*

R

radula 81
rainbow squid 76-7, 77, 78-9,
 78-9, 91
rainforest 10, *10,* 34
Rainshadow Desert 65, 80-3
rattleback 35, *35,* 91
reef 11, *11,* 42, 44, 93
reef glider 42, *43,* 45, *46,* 47, 91
reptile 12, 13, 19, 28-31, 50, 93
rhinoceros 35
rift valley 5, *5*
roachcutter 54, *54,* 91
rodent 27, 35, 93

S

salt flats 23, 28, *28, 29, 30-1,* 32
savannah 11
scorpion 13
scrofa 32, *32-3,* 91
seal 15
sea level 6, 40
sea slug 42, *42*
sea spider 47
shagrat 27, *27,* 91
Shallow Seas 41, 42-7
shark 15, *15,* 76, *76*

sharkopath 76, *76,* 91
shrimp 72
silver spider *61,* 62-3, *62-3,* 91
silverswimmer 72-3, *72-3,* 74, 77, 91
skeleton 12, 13
slickribbon 70, 71, *71,* 91
slug 13
snail 13, *13,* 81, *81*
snake 28
snowstalker 26-7, *26, 27,* 91
species 16-17, 22, 39, 72, 93
spider 13, *13,* 62-3, *62-3*
spindletrooper 47, *47,* 91
spitfire beetle 56, *57,* 91
spitfire bird 55, *55,* 91
squibbon 88, *88-9,* 91
squid 13, *13,* 77, 78, *78,* 87, 88, *88*
swampus 52-3, *52-3,* 91
symbiotic relationship 47, 93

T

tadpole 16
terabyte 66-9, *67, 68-9,* 91
termite 16, *66,* 67
toraton 50-1, *50-1,* 91
tornado 38, 93
torpor 38, 93
tortoise 51, *51*
tropics 9, *9*
tundra 10, *10,* 26-7, 93
turtle *18*

V

vampire bat 39, *39*
vertebrate 12, 18
volcano 4

W

walrus 10
warm blooded 12, 13
warning displays *30,* 56
wasp 56
whale *11*
worm 18, 70-1, *70, 71*

Z

zebra 14, *14*

A FIREFLY BOOK

Published by Firefly Books Ltd., 2003
Copyright © The Future is Wild™ 2003
The Future is Wild name and logo are registered trademarks
of The Future is Wild Ltd.

First Printing

National Library of Canada Cataloguing in Publication Data

Pye, Claire
    The wild world of the future / Claire Pye.
Includes index.
ISBN 1-55297-727-7 (bound).—ISBN 1-55297-725-0 (pbk)
    1. Evolution (Biology)—Forecasting—Juvenile literature.
I. Title.
QH367.1.P93 2003   j576.8   C2002-905272-6

Publisher Cataloging-in-Publication Data (U.S)
(Library of Congress Standards)

Pye, Claire.
    The wild world of the future / Claire Pye.—1st ed.
[96] p. : ill. , col. photos. ;   cm.
Includes index.
Summary: Based on evolutionary and biological principles,
what animals and the earth will look like 5 million years, 100
million and 200 million years from now.
Note: Companion book to the Discovery Channel series: The
Future is Wild.
ISBN 1-55297-727-7
ISBN 1-55297-725-0 (pbk.)
1. Earth evolution—Juvenile literature. 2. Earth—
Environmental aspects—Juvenile literature. 2. Global
warming—Environmental aspects—Juvenile literature.(1.
Earth evolution. 2. Earth—Environmental aspects. 3. Global
warming—Environmental aspects.) I. Title.
551.7 21   QE28.3.P94 2003

Published in Canada in 2003 by
Firefly Books Ltd.
3680 Victoria Park Avenue
Toronto, Ontario, M2H 3K1

Published in the United States in 2003 by
Firefly Books (U.S.) Inc.
P.O. Box 1338, Ellicott Station
Buffalo, New York 14205

This book and the associated television series
were conceived by The Future is Wild Ltd
Solomon's Court, Bournes Green, Stroud, GL6 8LY, UK
from an original idea by John Adams

Text consultant Professor R McNeill Alexander,
University of Leeds, UK
Researcher John Capener

This book was created by
act-two, 346 Old Street, London EC1V 9RB
www.act-two.com

Managing editor Deborah Kespert
Senior designer Liz Adcock
Author Claire Pye
Additional text Anna Claybourne
Editorial support Mark Blacklock, Paul Virr
Picture research Ellen Root
Illustrations Peter Bull Art Studio, Mel Pickering
Image retouching Itchy Animation
Digital artwork 422
Editorial director Jane Wilsher
Art director Belinda Webster
Production Heather O'Connell
Index Ann Barrett

Reproduction by Icon Reproduction, England
Printed in Italy